Longman exam practice kit

A-Level Chemistry

Michael C Cox

Philip J Barratt

LONGMAN

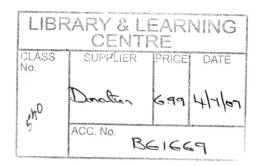
Acknowledgements
We are grateful to the Publishers, Addison Wesley Longman, and to the series editors, Geoff Black and Stuart Wall for inviting us to write this book and thereby giving us the opportunity to help students achieve their potential of really good grades in chemistry. We should like to thank our own students, past and present, for sharing our enthusiasm for chemistry. We also thank our many professional colleagues for sharing with us their expertise in teaching and testing chemistry. Above all we wish to thank our wives, Maureen and Maureen, for their continuing love, patience and support.
MCC & PJB

Series Editors
Geoff Black and Stuart Wall

Titles available
A-level
Biology
Business Studies
Chemistry
Mathematics
Psychology
Sociology

Addison Wesley Longman Ltd,
Edinburgh Gate, Harlow,
Essex CM20 2JE, England
and Associated Companies throughout the World.

First Published 1997

ISBN 0-582-30388-5

British Library Cataloguing-in-Publication Data
A catalogue record for this book is available from the British Library.

Printed in Great Britain by Henry Ling Ltd., at the Dorset Press, Dorchester, Dorset

Contents

Introduction iv

Part I   **Revising and preparing for examinations** 1

Part II   **Core chemistry topics and questions** 7

    Topic 1 Structure and bonding 8

    Topic 2 Energetics *15*

    Topic 3 Kinetics *22*

    Topic 4 Chemical equilibria *29*

    Topic 5 Electrochemistry and redox *36*

    Topic 6 The Periodic Table *43*

    Topic 7 Organic chemistry *53*

Part III   **Answers and tips for topics 1 to 7** 63

    Topic 1 Solutions: Structure and bonding 65

    Topic 2 Solutions: Energetics *67*

    Topic 3 Solutions: Kinetics *68*

    Topic 4 Solutions: Chemical equilibria *70*

    Topic 5 Solutions: Electrochemistry and redox *72*

    Topic 6 Solutions: The Periodic Table *74*

    Topic 7 Solutions: Organic chemistry *77*

Part IV   **Practice papers, answers and mark schemes** 81

    Paper 1 ($1\frac{1}{2}$ hr) General chemistry *82*

    Paper 2 ($1\frac{1}{4}$ hr) Inorganic chemistry *85*

    Paper 3 ($1\frac{1}{4}$ hr) Organic chemistry *87*

    Paper 4 (1 hr) Objective test *89*

    Solutions Paper 1 *93*

    Solutions Paper 2 *96*

    Solutions Paper 3 *99*

    Solutions Paper 4 *102*

Introduction

If you want to pass chemistry with really good grades then this is the book for you. You will discover how to:

▶ get the examiners on your side;
▶ answer questions correctly, and;
▶ get full marks for your answers.

This book is in four parts. Part I helps you to plan your revision and prepare for your exams. Part II covers the seven fundamental chemistry topics that examination boards must include in their A-level syllabuses. Each topic contains:

▶ **key points** for quick reference;
▶ **multiple choice questions** for quick revision;
▶ **structured questions** to test the topic, and;
▶ **helpful hints** and clues from examiners.

Part III gives you all the answers as well as detailed mark schemes, tips and other inside information from the examiners. Part IV contains practice examination papers for you to tackle against the clock. These questions test more than one topic in your chemistry syllabus. The answers, mark schemes and comments from examiners are provided so you can correct your work and monitor your progress.

MAKING THE MOST OF THIS BOOK

Reference Guide

Study Guide

We have designed this book for you to use. **Read it *and* write in it!**

Each topic begins with the key points. Scan these for a quick revision summary. Do this reading **before** you do any writing. If you need to look up more details, consult the Chemistry Reference Guide published by Longman. If you need more explanation and help, use the Chemistry Study Guide also published by Longman. One of us wrote both those books to help you help yourself.

When you have revised the topic and you are ready to tackle a question, set the alarm on your wristwatch, or on a clock, to go off after the same number of minutes as the total number of marks for the question. Look out for any of our hints and clues to help you with the questions in Part II. **Write your answers in the spaces provided on the page**. The number of lines or the amount of space is a rough guide to how much to write. The number of marks (shown in brackets) for each part of a question is a rough guide to how much time (in minutes) to spend on that part. When the alarm goes off, stop writing.

Answering questions is important, but only half the task. Marking your answers is the other half of the task and even more important. It certainly boosts our confidence when our answers are correct. But we probably learn more when we have to do corrections. We designed the questions in this book neither to catch you out nor to give you false confidence. Check all your answers carefully and if any are wrong, make sure you understand not only why they are wrong but also what the correct answer should be and why.

part I

Revising and preparing for examinations

Revising and preparing for examinations

PLANNING YOUR REVISION

Question: How long is a twenty-four hour day?
Answer: 24 hrs.

The question may be a joke but the answer is not funny. Each of us has twenty-four hours in the day. Our time is something we cannot afford to waste, give away or let other people steal. Some students are more successful than others simply because they look after their time and use it wisely. When revising and preparing for examinations you may feel the need to work harder. Before you decide to devote more time and effort to your chemistry, make sure you are working as efficiently as possible. Answer these questions:

1 Do you enjoy studying chemistry? yes ❏ no ❏
2 Do you have good study habits? yes ❏ no ❏
3 Do you follow a programme of spaced revision? yes ❏ no ❏
4 Do you regularly tackle chemistry questions? yes ❏ no ❏
5 Do you take practice papers under exam conditions? yes ❏ no ❏

We are usually better at subjects we like than at subjects we dislike. The more we like a subject the easier we find it and the more time we spend studying it. A habit is something that doesn't need great effort or will power. Good students never seem to have to think about studying because they habitually use good study techniques. Top students:

► do private study in the same place at the same times each day
► warm up at the start of each study session with a simple task
► work up gradually from easier to more difficult parts of a topic
► stop each study session while they are still enjoying success
► clear their table and leave a simple task to start their next session

Really good students never leave revision to the last minute. Various investigations and research have shown that top students always revise new material as soon as possible and they use frequent and short periods of revision that are carefully spaced. Tony Buzan, an expert on study techniques and author of the book *Make the Most of Your Mind*, recommends a pattern of spaced revision to follow a one-hour study session:

Study Guide
Chapter 2

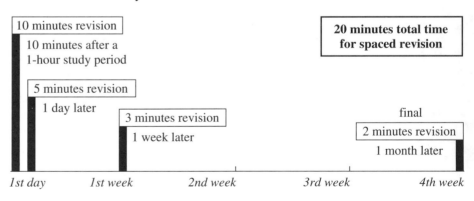

Really good students know the benefit of preparing for examinations by regularly tackling questions and practice papers and then correcting their answers very carefully.

GETTING TO GRIPS WITH EXAMINATION QUESTIONS

All the examination boards use structured questions. Some also use comprehension questions, essay or free-response questions and a variety of objective test questions: multiple choice, multiple completion and, in Scotland, grid questions. Most boards now offer modular examinations which often consist of several short papers composed of structured questions.

Study Guide
pages 7–11

Structured questions

A structured question consists of a number of parts, usually labelled (a), (b), (c), etc. A part may be subdivided into parts labelled (i), (ii), (iii), etc. Each part usually requires a short answer and the marks allocated to it are shown alongside the lines or space for the answer. Although you may often judge from the lines or space how much to write, you may sometimes be given a whole line for just a one-word answer. *Always use the marks to check how much time to spend on each part*.

When one part of a question is further divided into parts, the subdivisions (a)(i), (a)(ii), (a)(iii), etc., are usually linked together so that one part leads you on to the next. If these parts involve a calculation, they may lead you through the working in easy stages. Sometimes, **but not always**, a structured question is a stepped question in which successive parts become progressively more difficult. *Always quickly scan through an entire structured question before you tackle any of its parts*.

When one part of a question is worth two or more marks, you know that your answer must contain two or more points worth one mark each. However, sometimes your answer must contain two points for one mark: e.g. a correct numerical answer *without* the units may earn you no marks. And even with the correct units, your numerical answer might earn no marks if the number of significant figures is incorrect. So beware – examiners do not give half marks! *Always make sure that your answers are complete and appropriate*.

A structured question (or one of its parts) may begin with some data or information needed to answer some or all of the parts. You will see examples of this in Part II and Part IV of this book. Relative atomic mass (r.a.m.) values are often needed in a calculation. Examination boards may include them in a Periodic Table provided for the papers. They may also print these r.a.m. values on the front of the examination paper or, as we have done, at an appropriate place in the question. The data and information could give you strong clues to the examiner's thinking and the answer required. *Always check the information provided and make appropriate use of the data supplied*.

The Welsh Joint Education Committee publishes its chemistry examination papers in English and in Welsh. All other boards, including the Scottish Examination Board, publish their papers in English. In spite of this, examination candidates have sometimes complained that they knew the answer but just didn't understand the question! Here is a list of words and phrases most frequently used by the boards in their structured papers. *Always read the question carefully and answer the question being asked*.

The examiner's language

► **Concise answers with the bare minimum of detail:**
  – *Classify* each of the following oxides as acidic, basic or amphoteric.
  – *Define* the term molar first ionization energy.
  – *Give* the oxidation number of uranium in the compound.

- – *Indicate* the conditions needed to increase the equilibrium yield.
- – *Name* the type of mechanism in the reaction of ammonia with bromoethane.
- – *State* Hess's law.
- – *What is meant by* a buffer solution?
- – *Write* a balanced equation for the complete combustion of ethanol.
▶ Concise answers with essential but rather more detail:
  - – *Calculate* the activation energy from the data provided.
  - – *Comment* on the difference in physical properties of CO_2 and SiO_2.
  - – *Deduce* the structure of the compound from the information provided.
  - – *Draw* a labelled Born-Haber cycle for the formation of calcium oxide.
  - – *Identify* the compounds X, Y and Z in the following observations.
  - – *Outline* a laboratory method of measuring a named enthalpy change.
  - – *Show how you would* detect the presence of sodium in a compound.
  - – *Sketch* the unit cell of a body-centred cubic structure.
▶ Longer reasoned answers supported by relevant facts and principles:
  - – *Explain why* ammonia is basic and can form complexes with metal cations.
  - – *Explain what is meant by* fractional distillation.
  - – *State and explain* the effect of temperature upon reaction rates.
  - – *Suggest* a way to distinguish between 1-bromobutane and 2-bromobutane.

What are examiners looking for?

Examiners set questions to test your knowledge and understanding of the fundamental facts, patterns, principles and theories of chemistry. They will also test your ability to

▶ write and balance equations
▶ do calculations (pH, ΔH, K_c, E, etc.)
▶ predict the feasibility of reactions
▶ deduce organic structures

This book concentrates on these fundamentals to help you achieve the top grade. We have used our knowledge, skill and experience to provide you with a range of structured questions and objective test questions to cover the core topics in chemistry. We tailored the questions in Part II specifically to suit each topic so that you can revise and test yourself on the topics in any order you choose. We suggest that you answer, mark and correct only one structured question per study period. Use the key points to revise **before** (but **not** as) you tackle a question. *Always commit yourself to paper by writing your answers in the spaces provided in this book.*

You could use the multiple choice, multiple completion and grid questions for quick revision especially when you only have a short study period. You should use the questions in Part IV to set yourself practice examination papers under the strictly timed conditions indicated by the total number of marks for the paper.

Instructions for objective test questions

A multiple choice question is a question (or incomplete statement) followed by four suggested answers (or completing statements) labelled **A** to **D**. You have to select the **one** letter for the correct answer (or best completing statement). A multiple completion question has four *numbered* answers (or completing statements) one, two or three of which may be correct (or suitable). You have to select the **one** letter from **A** to **D** according to the following rules:

    A if (i), (ii) and (iii) only are correct (or suitable)
    B if (i) and (iii) only are correct (or suitable)
    C if (ii) and (iv) only are correct (or suitable)
    D if (iv) only is correct (or suitable)

One or more grid questions follow a grid (of six cells labelled **A** to **F**) containing answers or statements. You answer each question by selecting **one or more** letters from **A** to **F**. When you answer any type of objective test question, obey the instructions and always check that the letters you are choosing match the question you are answering.

HOW TO TAKE EXAMINATIONS

When you set yourself a practice paper, treat it seriously like the real thing. Persuade a relative or friend to supervise your examination by starting you off, keeping an eye on you and telling you when to stop. Finally, here is some really good advice from the Longman Chemistry Study Guide. It is well worth repeating.

► The first thing to do is prepare yourself thoroughly. Check the syllabus to see what you will need to take into the examination room. And check the regulations to see what you are allowed to take in. For example, different boards have different regulations about calculators. Some do not allow you to use a calculator in the OT paper. If you are allowed a calculator, it must be silent, cordless and unable to store and display text or graphics. If the calculator is programmable, you must clear the memory of any programs – and you cannot take the calculator instruction manual into the examination room.

► Tackle at least one set of past papers. Use the number of marks and the time allowed for each paper to calculate the *mark rate:* it is often about 1 mark per minute. Take off your wristwatch and put it in front of you where you can see it clearly. Get into the habit of checking your watch to keep to time. Do not spend too long on one question and not enough time on another. Time lost can rarely be recovered. Misjudging the time is one of the common mistakes you must avoid. If you are running out of time towards the end of an examination, abandon sentences and write your answers in note form.

► Allow yourself at least one minute before the end of an OT paper to check through your answer grid to make sure you have attempted every question. You will score zero for any question you omit but you will NOT score −1 for a wrong choice. So a guess is better than nothing. In an OT paper, you must follow the precise instructions for correcting any mistake you may make. If you mark more than one choice you will score zero for that particular question. In all other written papers if you think you have made a mistake, cross it out neatly with one ruled line. Do not use an 'erasable pen' and do not use white correcting fluid (boards forbid it). Examiners look at your 'mistakes' and are sometimes allowed to award you marks for what you have crossed out.

A FINAL WORD OF ADVICE

Don't put off until tomorrow what you can do today. Use this book throughout your course of study. Use it in conjunction with the Longman Reference Guide and the Study Guide. And when your examination is only 12 weeks away, start using the Longman Revision Planner that is included with this book.

Good Luck from us both.   MCC & PJB

1 *Structure and bonding*

Study Guide
Chapter 3

TOPIC OUTLINE

Atomic structure

Atoms

▶ **Atomic number** *(Z)* Number of protons in the nucleus of an atom or ion *or* number of electrons in the neutral atom

▶ **Mass number** *(A)* Number of protons *and* neutrons in the nucleus

Isotopes

Atoms with the same atomic number (Z) but different mass numbers (A)
Example $^{35}_{17}Cl$ $^{37}_{17}Cl$ $Z = 17$, $A = 35$ and 37

Radioactive isotope

Nucleus of unstable atom disintegrates to form new element by:

α-*radiation (helium nuclei)*	β-*radiation (electrons)*
Z decreases by 2 and A decreases by 4 to give a new element two places to the left in the Periodic Table	Z increases by 1 and A stays unchanged to give a new element one place to the right in the Periodic Table
$^{235}_{92}U \rightarrow {}^{231}_{90}Th + \alpha$	$^{14}_{6}C \rightarrow {}^{14}_{7}N + \beta$

Radioactive decay

First order process with constant half-life (carbon dating with ^{14}C).

Relative atomic mass (A$_r$)

Ratio of average mass per atom of the natural isotopic composition of an element to one-twelfth of the mass of an atom of the nuclide ^{12}C.

Electronic configurations

Ground state electronic configurations:

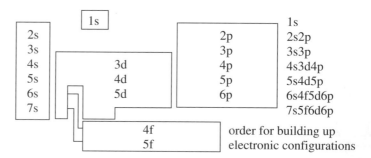

The numbers 1, 2, 3, 4, etc., are sometimes called the *principal quantum numbers*. The terms s, p, d and f denote *orbitals* each with 0, 1 or 2 (maximum) electrons.

type of orbital	s	p	d	f
maximum number of orbitals in shell	1	3	5	7
maximum total of electrons	2	6	10	14

For orbitals of the same energy, electrons occupy them singly before pairing up. For the d orbitals there is particular stability when half-filled (5 electrons) or completely filled (10 electrons): see *Topic 6* (chemistry of transition elements).

Bonding

Octet rule
Atoms have a tendency on bonding to achieve noble gas electronic configurations. Elements in the Period Lithium to Neon have a maximum covalency of 4. Elements in the other Periods can expand their octet and show a covalency greater than 4.

Ionic bonding
Result of *electrons being transferred* from one atom (usually a metal) to another atom (usually a non-metal) and oppositely charged ions being packed into a crystal lattice.
▶ **Anion polarization** Distortion of the shape of a polarizable anion by a polarizing cation. Polarizability increases with increasing charge and size of the anion.
▶ **Cation polarizing power** Ability to distort the shape of a polarizable anion. Polarizing power increases with increasing charge and decreasing size of the cation.
▶ **Covalent character of an ionic compound** is high if the cation is small, the anion is large and the charges on the ions are high.

Covalent bonding
Result of a pair of *electrons being shared* between two atoms because their nuclei attract the electrons more strongly than they repel one another: H—H
▶ **Dative (coordinate) bond** Two electrons shared by two atoms, one (the donor atom) supplying both electrons to share with the other (the acceptor atom): $H_3N{:}{\rightarrow}BCl_3$.
▶ **Pauling electronegativity index (N_p)** A measure of how strongly an atom in a compound attracts electrons in a bond (see *Topic 6* – trends in electronegativity).

▶ **Polar covalent bond** Result of unequal sharing of electrons between atoms with different electronegativities.
▶ **Hydrated cations** Result of dative bond with the donor oxygen atom (in the water molecules) and the acceptor ion (see *Topic 6* – transition metal complexes).

▶ **Delocalized bonding** Result of shared valence electrons distributed over three or more atoms instead of confined to being shared between two atoms (six electrons shared between six carbon atoms in benzene): see *Topic 7*.

Metallic bonding
Net attraction resulting from mutually repelling positive ions being held together by their attraction for a 'sea' of mobile delocalized electrons.

Hydrogen bonding (X—H·····Y)
Weak bond (·····) of an electrostatic nature between an electronegative atom (Y = N, O or F) and a hydrogen covalently bonded to an electronegative atom (X = N, O or F).

van der Waals forces
Weak short range instantaneously induced dipole–dipole attractions operating between atoms **in all substances**. Increases with number of electrons in atoms: e.g. the b.pt. of noble gases increases from He to Xe.

Study Guide
Chapter 4

Structure

Coordination number
Number of nearest equidistant neighbouring particles.

Metallic structures
Most metals have a coordination number of 12: *hexagonal* and *cubic* (*close-packed*). Alkali metals have a coordination number of 8: *body-centred* (not close-packed).

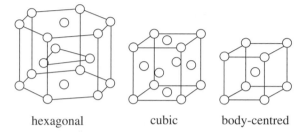

hexagonal   cubic   body-centred

Ionic crystals
CsCl double simple cubic; NaCl face-centred cubic. (see page 66)
Radius ratio Radius of smaller ion divided by radius of larger ion.

coordination number:	8	6	4
radius ratio:	>0.73	<0.73 and >0.41	<0.41

Giant covalent structures

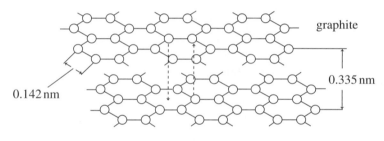

graphite

0.335 nm

0.142 nm

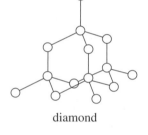

diamond

silicon carbide

VSEPR
(Valence Shell Electron Pair Repulsion) theory to predict the shape of simple covalent molecules on the basis of repulsion between electron-pairs.

non-bonded/non-bonded pairs > bonded/non-bonded pairs > bonded/bonded pairs

N.B. A non-bonded pair of electrons may also be called a *lone pair* of electrons.

Polar molecule
The shape of the molecule allows polar bonds to reinforce each other.

Non-polar molecule
No polar bonds, or the shape of the molecule causes two or more polar bonds to cancel each other.

$$\overset{\delta-}{O}=\overset{\delta+\delta+}{C}=\overset{\delta-}{O}$$

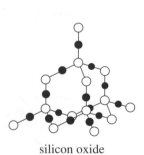

silicon oxide

★ REVISION ACTIVITY

Multiple choice questions

1. Which one of the following represents the most polar molecule?
   A H—Br   B H—Cl   C H—F   D H—I   ✓

2. Which one of the following best describes the structure of caesium chloride?
   A body-centred cubic   C double simple cubic   ✓
   B cubic close-packed   D hexagonal close-packed

3. Which one of the following is responsible for the boiling point of the halogens increasing with increasing atomic number?
   A covalent bonding   C ion–dipole forces   ✓
   B hydrogen bonding   D van der Waals forces

4. Which pair of elements would be expected to form the compound with the most ionic character?
   A Cs and F   B Li and I   C Cs and I   D Li and F   ✗

5. The first eight standard molar ionisation energies (in $kJ\,mol^{-1}$) of an element X are 1000   2200   3400   4600   7000   8500   27000   32000. Which one of the following would best represent the formula of its aqueous ion?
   A X^+ B X^{2+} C X^{2-} D X^- ✗

$\dfrac{3}{5}$

Grid question

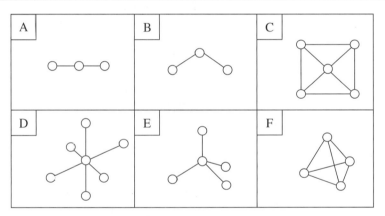

Identify the shape of:
✓ E (a) an ammonium ion   (c) a tetraaquacopper(II) ion   C ✓
✓ B (b) a nitrogen dioxide molecule   (d) an aqueous hydrogen ion   A ✗ F

$\dfrac{3}{4}$

Multiple completion question

answer choice
A = (i)(ii)(iii)
B = (i)(iii)
C = (ii)(iv)
D = (iv)

Which of the following would represent the ground state electronic configuration for an atom of an element in the s-block of the Periodic Table?
   (i) $1s^2 2s^2 2p^6 3s^2 3p^2$
   (ii) $1s^2 2s^2 2p^6 3s^2 3p^6 4s^1$
   (iii) $1s^2 2s^2 2p^6 3s^2 3p^6 3d^{10} 4s^2$
   (iv) $1s^2 2s^2 2p^6 3s^2 3p^6 3d^{10} 4s^2 4p^6 5s^2$

C ✓

$\dfrac{7}{10}$

EXAMINATION QUESTIONS

Question 1

(a) Explain the difference between *mass number* and *relative atomic mass*.

....

....

....

....

....

.... [3]

HINT

Do you add or multiply probabilities together?

(b) Chlorine contains two isotopes ^{35}Cl and ^{37}Cl in the ratio of 3:1.

(i) What is the probability of an atom of chlorine being ^{35}Cl?

3/4 or 75%

.... [1]

(ii) What is the probability of a molecule of chlorine containing two ^{35}Cl atoms?

0.75 × 0.75 = 0.5625

.... [1]

(iii) What is the probability of a molecule of chlorine containing two ^{37}Cl atoms?

0.25 × 0.25 = 0.0625

.... [1]

(iv) From your answers to (ii) and (iii), state the probability of a molecule of chlorine containing one ^{35}Cl atom and one ^{37}Cl atom.

1 - (0.5625 + 0.0625) = 0.375

.... [1]

(v) Sketch the mass spectrum of chlorine in the molecular ion region showing clearly the relative heights of the peaks.

height of peak

69   70   71   72   73   74   75   mass/charge ratio [2]

(c) Radioactive ^{14}C is a beta emitter with a half-life of 5600 years. It is assimilated by all living organisms and its radioactivity is constant while the organism is alive. When an organism dies, no more ^{14}C is taken up and the radioactivity due to ^{14}C begins to fall.

(i) Write an equation to represent the radioactive decay of an atom of ^{14}C.

.... [2]

(ii) If a wooden archaeological artefact has a ^{14}C activity of 12.5% that of a living tree, what is the approximate age of the artefact?

halflife = 50%, 2·halflife = 25%, 3·halflife = 12.5% ∴

.... [2]

total 13 marks

approx age of artefact
= 56000 × 3
= 16 800 yrs old.

Question 2

(a) Write the ground state electronic configurations, in terms of s, p and d electrons, for each of the following isolated species:

17   (i) a chlorine atom..... $1s^2\ 2s^2\ 2p^6\ 3s^2\ 3p^5$ .....

20   (ii) a calcium ion..... $1s^2\ 2s^2\ 2p^6\ 3s^2\ 3p^6\ 4s^2$ .....

24   (iii) a chromium atom..... $1s^2\ 2s^2\ 2p^6\ 3s^2\ 3p^6\ 4s^1\ 3d^5$ ..... [3]

(b) Draw dot and cross diagrams to represent the following covalent molecules:

(i) ammonia, NH_3

HINT
Remember the lone pairs!

[1]

(ii) carbon dioxide, CO_2

[1]

(iii) aluminium chloride, Al_2Cl_6

[2]

(c) (i) Describe the **difference** between the structures of sodium chloride and caesium chloride. Your answer may be *either* a written description *or* clearly labelled diagrams.

....

....

....

....

....

....

....

....

....

....

....

....

.... [4]

(ii) Give a reason why sodium chloride and caesium chloride have different structures.

....

.... [1]

total 12 marks

Question 3
(a) Complete the following table.

Molecule	Number of bonding electron pairs	Number of non-bonding electron pairs	Shape of molecule
BF_3			trigonal planar
NH_3	3	1	
SF_6		0	
H_2O	2	2	bent

[4]

(b) MX_2Y_2 is the general formula for an ionic or molecular compound. Draw labelled diagrams to explain why the ions or molecules can exist in two forms if their structure is square planar but only in one form if their structure is tetrahedral.

[3]

HINT
What words are in bold letters?

(c) Diamond and solid iodine are both covalent crystals.
   (i) State **two** differences in their **physical** properties.

....

.... [2]

   (ii) Explain the difference in their physical properties in terms of the forces between atoms and molecules.

....

....

....

....

.... [3]

total 12 marks

2 Energetics

■ **TOPIC OUTLINE** ■

Energy changes

Study Guide
Chapter 6

Heat change (δq)
mass (m) $\times$ specific heat capacity (c) $\times$ change in temperature (δt)
δq = (heat content of products − heat content of reactants);
$c \approx 4.2\,\mathrm{J\,g^{-1}\,K^{-1}}$ for aqueous solutions;
δt = (final temperature − initial temperature).

Enthalpy change (δH)
Heat change *at constant pressure*.

Molar enthalpy change (ΔH)
Heat change *per mole* **at constant pressure**.

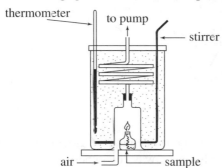

Flame calorimeter
measures heats
of combustion
at constant pressure

Molar internal energy change (ΔU)
Heat change *per mole* **at constant volume**.

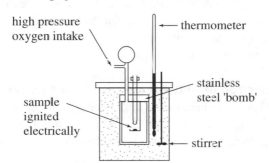

Bomb calorimeter
measures heats
of combustion
at constant volume

$\Delta H = \Delta U + \Delta n \,.\, RT$
where R is the gas constant ($8.3\,\mathrm{J\,mol^{-1}\,K^{-1}}$), T is the temperature in kelvin and Δn is (number of moles gaseous products − number of moles gaseous reactants).

Standard Molar Enthalpy Change ($\Delta H^{\ominus}$)
Refers to reactants and products at 298 K and 101 kPa (1 atm) with solution concentrations of $1.00\,\mathrm{mol\,dm^{-3}}$.

Reference Guide
for definitions

▶ *Exothermic reactions* Values of ΔH are **negative**.
▶ *Endothermic reactions* Values of ΔH are **positive**.

First law of thermodynamics
Energy cannot be created and cannot be destroyed.

Hess's law
The standard molar enthalpy change of a process is independent of the
means or route by which the process takes place.

Standard Enthalpy Changes
▶ $\Delta H_{c,298}^{\ominus}$ (*combustion*) one mole of substance (at 298 K and 1 atm) completely
burnt in oxygen to form products (at 298 K and 1 atm): always exothermic.
▶ $\Delta H_{f,298}^{\ominus}$ (*formation*) one mole of a compound (at 298 K and 1 atm) is formed
from its constituent elements in their most stable form at 298 K and 1 atm.
$$\Delta H_{f,298}^{\ominus} = \Delta H_{c,298}^{\ominus} \text{ (compound)} - \Sigma \Delta H_{c,298}^{\ominus} \text{ (constituent elements)}$$
▶ $\Delta H_{r,298}^{\ominus}$ for a reaction represented by a balanced chemical equation specifying
the stoichiometric amounts of reactants and products.
$$\Delta H_{r,298}^{\ominus} = \Sigma \Delta H_{f,298}^{\ominus} \text{ (products)} - \Sigma \Delta H_{f,298}^{\ominus} \text{ (reactants)}$$
Cycle to calculate enthalpy changes

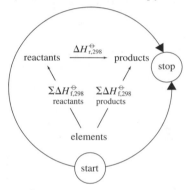

▶ $\Delta H_{a,298}^{\ominus}$ (*atomization*) one mole of gaseous atoms formed from the element under
standard conditions: always endothermic.

Ionization energy
May be defined as the molar energy change for the process
$X^{n+}(g) \rightarrow X^{(n+1)+}(g) + e^{-}(g)$ where n is zero (first ionization energy) or a positive integer (n = 1, 2, 3, ... for 2nd, 3rd, 4th, ... ionization energy). Plot of molar
first ionization energies against atomic number sheds light on the electronic
structures of the elements.

Electron affinity (or electron-gain energy)
May be defined as the molar energy change for the process
$Y^{n-}(g) + e^{-}(g) \rightarrow Y^{(n+1)-}(g)$ where n is zero or a positive integer. 1st electron-
gain energy for oxygen is exothermic: 2nd is endothermic.

Bond energy (enthalpy) $E(X—Y)$
The *average* standard enthalpy change to break a mole of bonds in a gaseous
molecule to form gaseous atoms.

Bond breaking is always endothermic
Bond energies range from about 150 kJ mol^{-1} for weak bonds (e.g. F—F) to
$350–550 \text{ kJ mol}^{-1}$ for strong bonds (e.g. C—C) to around 1000 kJ mol^{-1} for very
strong bonds (e.g. N $\equiv$ N). Bond energy increases with number of electron pairs
shared (e.g. $E(C \equiv C) > E(C{=}C) > E(C—C)$. See *Topic 6* – trends in properties
of hydrogen halides.

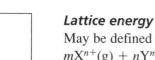

Reference Guide
for definitions

Lattice energy

May be defined as the standard molar internal energy for the process
$mX^{n+}(g) + nY^{m-}(g) \rightarrow X_mY_n(s)$ which is *exothermic* so values are *negative*.

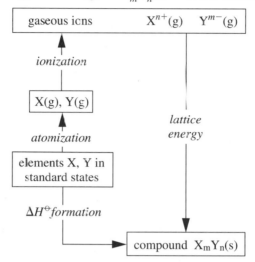

▶ Lattice energies for doubly-charged ions are usually more exothermic than those for singly-charged ions.

▶ Lattice energies become less exothermic as ion size increases (charge density decreases).

Lattice-breaking enthalpy

May be defined as the standard molar enthalpy change for the process
$X_mY_n(s) \rightarrow mX^{n+}(g) + nY^{m-}(g)$ which is *endothermic* so values are *positive*.

Heats of solution

▶ May be *exothermic* or *endothermic* and are usually small differences between two large values: lattice-breaking enthalpy and hydration enthalpy.

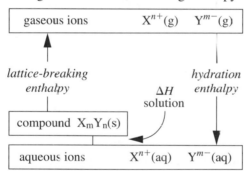

▶ The enthalpy change of a solution depends on the amount of solvent used. Data books give values for infinite dilution.

Standard molar free energy change ($\Delta G^{\ominus}$)

A reaction will be *spontaneous* (*energetically feasible*) if its standard molar free energy change has a *negative value*.

Entropy

A measure of the random dispersal of energy of a system.
$\Delta G^{\ominus} = \Delta G^{\ominus} - T . \Delta S^{\ominus}$ where $\Delta S^{\ominus}$ is the standard molar entropy change.
$\Delta S^{\ominus}$ (total) = $\Delta S^{\ominus}$ (surroundings) + $\Delta S^{\ominus}$ (system)

Second law of thermodynamics

Total entropy always increases if a spontaneous reaction occurs.

REVISION ACTIVITY

Multiple choice questions

1 Which one of the following changes is measured experimentally in a bomb calorimeter?
　　A　enthalpy ΔH　　　　　　　　C　free energy ΔG
　　B　entropy ΔS　　　　　　　　　D　internal energy ΔU

2 For which one of the following processes is the enthalpy change **always** positive?
　　A　atomization　　　　　　　　　C　formation
　　B　combustion　　　　　　　　　D　neutralization

3 Which of the following probably has the largest negative value for the lattice energy as defined by the process $mX^{n+}(g) + nY^{m-}(g) \rightarrow X_mY_n(s)$?
　　A　LiI　　　　　B　CsF　　　　C　MgF_2　　　　D　MgI_2

4 If the enthalpy change for $NaCl(s) \rightarrow Na^+(g) + Cl^-(g)$ is $+787\,kJ\,mol^{-1}$ and the hydration enthalpies of Na^+ and Cl^- are $-406\,kJ\,mol^{-1}$ and $-377\,kJ\,mol^{-1}$ respectively, which one of the following is the solution enthalpy for $NaCl(s) \rightarrow NaCl(aq)$?
　　A　$+1570\,kJ\,mol^{-1}$　　　　　C　$-1570\,kJ\,mol^{-1}$
　　B　$+4\,kJ\,mol^{-1}$　　　　　　　D　$-4\,kJ\,mol^{-1}$

5 If the standard enthalpies of combustion of carbon, hydrogen and ethyne, C_2H_2, are respectively $-394\,kJ\,mol^{-1}$, $-286\,kJ\,mol^{-1}$ and $-1300\,kJ\,mol^{-1}$, which one of the following would be the enthalpy of formation of ethyne?
　　A　$+60\,kJ\,mol^{-1}$　　　　　　C　$-60\,kJ\,mol^{-1}$
　　B　$+226\,kJ\,mol^{-1}$　　　　　　D　$-226\,kJ\,mol^{-1}$

Grid question

In the grid δT is the rise in temperature and δH is the heat given off when $25\,cm^3$ of $1.0\,mol\,dm^{-3}$ HCl(aq) are added to $25\,cm^3$ of $1.0\,mol\,dm^{-3}$ NaOH(aq).

A δT would be less	B δT would be the same	C δT would be more
D δH would be less	E δH would be the same	F δH would be more

(a) Identify the most likely effect of using $50\,cm^3$ of acid and alkali instead of $25\,cm^3$

(b) Identify the most likely effect of using $CH_3CO_2H(aq)$ instead of HCl(aq)

Multiple completion question

answer choice
A = (i)(ii)(iii)
B = (i)(iii)
C = (ii)(iv)
D = (iv)

Which of the following bond energies would **NOT** be needed to calculate the enthalpy change for the reaction $CH_3CHO + H_2 \rightarrow CH_3CH_2OH$?
　(i) $E(C-H)$
　(ii) $E(C=O)$
　(iii) $E(C-O)$
　(iv) $E(C-C)$

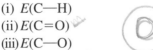

EXAMINATION QUESTIONS

Question 1

A student attempted to measure the enthalpy change of combustion of ethanol using the apparatus shown in the diagram.

(a) Suggest **four** improvements that could be made to the apparatus to get a more accurate result.

....

....

....

.... [4]

(b) The student's results were as follows:

thermometer
(−5 to +110 °C)

copper calorimeter

water

gauze on a tripod

flame

wick

ethanol

HINT (1 a)

Where should all the heat go?

Mass of empty calorimeter	= 120 g
Mass of water in calorimeter	= 100 g
Mass of ethanol, wick and container before experiment	= 43.56 g
Mass of ethanol, wick and container after experiment	= 41.36 g
Initial temperature of water in calorimeter	= 20 °C
Final temperature of water	= 75 °C
Specific heat capacity of copper	= 0.387 J g^{-1} K^{-1}
Specific heat capacity of water	= 4.18 J g^{-1} K^{-1}
Molar mass of ethanol	= 46.1 g mol^{-1}

(i) Use the above results to calculate a value for the molar enthalpy change of combustion of ethanol.

....

....

....

.... [4]

(ii) The data book value for the standard molar enthalpy change of combustion of ethanol is −1367 kJ mol^{-1}. Suggest reasons why the value calculated from the student's results differs from the value in the data book.

....

....

....

.... [4]

(c) Explain why a bomb calorimeter is used for accurate determinations of enthalpy changes and why the heat change measured is not an enthalpy change.

....

....

.... [3]

total 15 marks

Question 2

The following experiment was used to determine the molar enthalpy change of neutralization of hydrochloric acid and aqueous sodium hydroxide, each of concentration 2.0 mol dm^{-3}.

100 cm^3 of the acid at room temperature were placed in a glass beaker and 100 cm^3 of the alkali at the same temperature were placed in a polystyrene beaker of negligible thermal capacity. The temperature of the solution in the polystyrene beaker was recorded at half minute intervals before and after rapidly adding, with stirring, the 100 cm^3 of acid. The results are shown on the graph below.

HINT
Have you got your ruler?

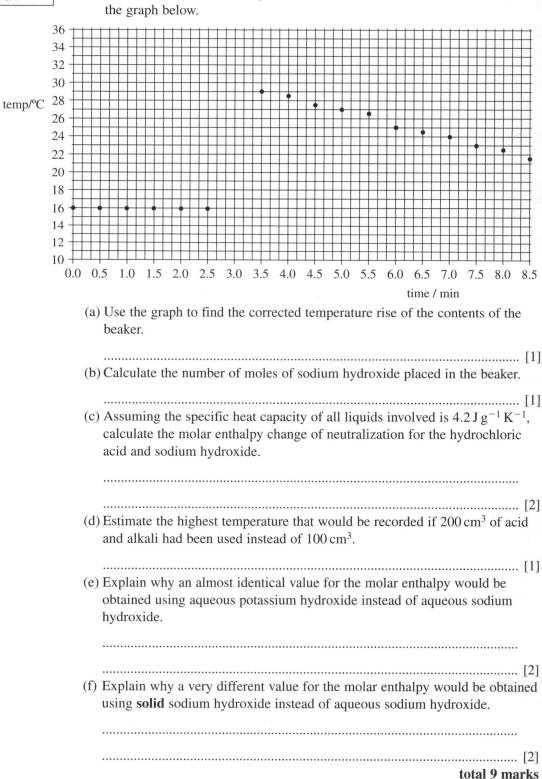

(a) Use the graph to find the corrected temperature rise of the contents of the beaker.

.... [1]

(b) Calculate the number of moles of sodium hydroxide placed in the beaker.

.... [1]

(c) Assuming the specific heat capacity of all liquids involved is 4.2 J g^{-1} K^{-1}, calculate the molar enthalpy change of neutralization for the hydrochloric acid and sodium hydroxide.

....

.... [2]

(d) Estimate the highest temperature that would be recorded if 200 cm^3 of acid and alkali had been used instead of 100 cm^3.

.... [1]

(e) Explain why an almost identical value for the molar enthalpy would be obtained using aqueous potassium hydroxide instead of aqueous sodium hydroxide.

....

.... [2]

(f) Explain why a very different value for the molar enthalpy would be obtained using **solid** sodium hydroxide instead of aqueous sodium hydroxide.

....

.... [2]

total 9 marks

Question 3

(a) The data book value for the standard molar enthalpy change of combustion ($\Delta H_{c,298}^{\ominus}$) of methane is given as $-890.3 \, \text{kJ mol}^{-1}$. A value for the enthalpy change of combustion of methane may be calculated from standard molar enthalpy changes of formation ($\Delta H_{f,298}^{\ominus}$) or from bond dissociation energies (E).

(i) Calculate the enthalpy change of combustion of methane using the following values for the standard molar enthalpy changes of formation.

compound	$\Delta H_{f,298}^{\ominus}$ / kJ mol^{-1}
carbon dioxide	-394
water	-286
methane	-74.8

....

....

.... [2]

(ii) Calculate the enthalpy change of combustion of methane using the following values for the average bond dissociation energies.

bond	E / kJ mol^{-1}
C—H	$+435$
O=O	$+498$
C=O	$+805$
H—O	$+464$

....

....

.... [2]

(iii) Comment upon the values calculated in (i) and (ii) above.

....

....

.... [2]

(b) Calculate the enthalpy change of solution of solid sodium chloride from the following data.

Change	Enthalpy change / kJ mol^{-1}
$NaCl(s) \rightarrow Na^+(g) + Cl^-(g)$	$+787$
$Cl^-(g) + aq \rightarrow Cl^-(aq)$	-377
$Na^+(g) + aq \rightarrow Na^+(aq)$	-406

....

....

.... [2]

total 8 marks

HINT

It's easier with a cycle!

3 *Kinetics*

◉ TOPIC OUTLINE

Study Guide
Chapter 9

Chemical kinetics

The study of reaction rates and of the influence of concentration, pressure, temperature and catalysts upon reaction rates.

Rates and concentration

During any chemical reaction the concentrations of reactants decrease and the concentrations of products increase.

Rate of reaction

Change of concentration in a given interval of time.

Units of rate are usually (but not always) $mol\,dm^{-3}\,s^{-1}$.

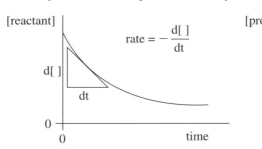
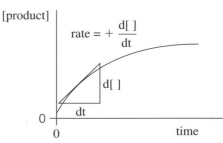

Determining rates

Reactions may be followed by measuring the concentration of a reactant or product (*sampling and titrimetry*) or by monitoring changes in a property of the system: e.g. mass, gas volume or pressure, liquid volume (*dilatometry*), colour intensity (*colorimetry*), rotation of the plane of polarized light (*polarimetry*).

Rate equations

Mathematical relationships between concentration and time. All rate equations must be determined experimentally: they cannot be predicted from stoichiometric equations.

Differential rate equations

Express rate as a function of concentration.

$$-d[\ ]/dt = k[A]^m[B]^n$$

where k is the proportionality constant, called the rate constant. m and n are the orders of reaction with respect to reactant A and reactant B.

Rate constant (k)

Value depends upon temperature but **not** upon concentration.

Overall order of a reaction ($m + n$)

Sum of the orders w.r.t. each reactant.

Integrated rate equations

Express concentration as a function of time.

▶ **Zero order reaction** $-d[\ ]/dt = k_0[\text{reactant}]^0$ $[\text{reactant}] = -k_0t + [\text{initial}]$

Rate independent of concentration.

Value for rate constant k_0 may be obtained from slope of graph of concentration against time.

Units of k_0 are $\text{mol dm}^{-3}\,\text{s}^{-1}$. Half-life $t_{1/2} = [\ ]/2k_0$.

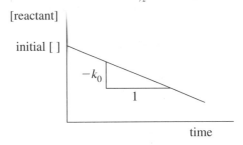

▶ **First order reaction** $-d[\ ]/dt = k_1[\text{reactant}]^1$ $\ln[\text{reactant}] = -k_1t + \ln[\text{initial}]$

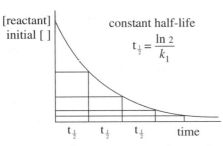
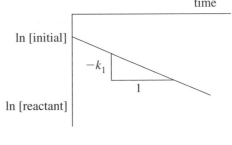

Value for rate constant k_1 may be obtained from slope of graph of ln concentration against time or from the half-life which is independent of concentration.

Units of $k_1 = \text{s}^{-1}$. Half-life $t_{1/2} = (\ln 2)/k_1$.

▶ **Second order reaction** $d[\ ]/dt = k_2[\text{reactant}]^2$ $1/[\text{reactant}] = k_2t + 1/[\text{initial}]$

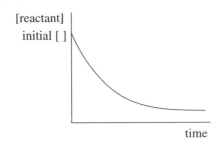
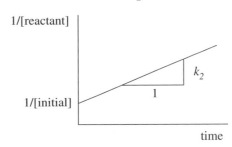

Value for rate constant k_2 may be obtained from slope of graph of 1/concentration against time. Units of k_2 are $\text{mol}^{-1}\,\text{dm}^3\,\text{s}^{-1}$ Half-life $t_{1/2} = 1/(k_2[\ ])$

N.B. The *amount of product* formed in any reaction always depends upon the *amounts of reactants* even though the rate of reaction may be independent of the concentration of a particular reactant simply because reactants react to produce products.

Reaction mechanism

A sequence of simple steps proposed in theory to account for the overall chemical reaction that takes place. The *slowest step* in a reaction mechanism is called the *rate-determining step* because it controls the overall rate of the reaction. The *order(s) of a reaction* may provide clues to the mechanism.

Rates and temperature

Arrhenius equation

$k = Ae^{-E_a/RT}$ or $\ln k = \ln A - E_a/RT$
A is the Arrhenius or pre-exponential factor
E_a is the activation energy for the reaction.

Activation energy (E_a)

A value (always positive) for E_a may be found from a graph of $\ln k$ against $1/T$ whose slope (negative) $= -E_a/R$. If gas constant (R) is $8.3\,\text{J}\,\text{K}^{-1}\,\text{mol}^{-1}$, then activation energy units will be $\text{J}\,\text{mol}^{-1}$. E_a may be seen as an energy barrier. The energy needed to break covalent bonds may in part explain why many organic reactions are slow.

Catalysis

Use of catalysts to alter the rate of a reaction.
▶ **Heterogeneous catalysts** are in a different physical state from the reactants and often function by surface absorption.
▶ **Homogeneous catalysts** are in the same physical state as the reactants and usually involve intermediate compound formation.
▶ Catalysts speed up the *rate of attainment of equilibrium* for reversible reactions but do **not** alter the equilibrium compositions.
▶ Catalysts take part in a reaction mechanism but are not consumed by the reaction, therefore they do not appear as reactants in the equation for the overall reaction. They provide *alternative reaction pathways with lower activation energies* than those for uncatalysed reactions. The effect of a catalyst may be shown in an energy diagram.

Energy profile diagram

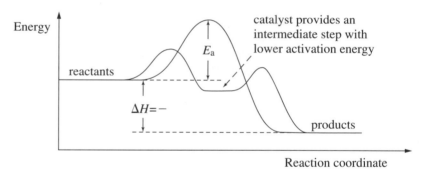

Energy distribution diagram

As a factor in the Arrhenius equation, E_a determines the proportion of reacting species having enough energy to cross the activation energy barrier.

f(E,n) is a function of energy distribution such that the total area under the curve of f(E,n) against energy is proportional to the total number of reactant species.

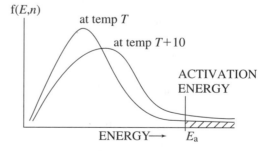

Effect of temperature on reaction rate

The area under the curve to the right of E_a and, therefore, the number of molecules colliding with enough energy to cause a reaction roughly doubles for every ten degree rise in temperature.

★ **REVISION ACTIVITY**

Multiple choice questions

1 For the iodination of aqueous propanone:

$$CH_3COCH_3 + I_2 \rightarrow CH_2ICOCH_3 + H^+ + I^-,$$

the rate equation is $-\dfrac{d[I]}{dt} = k[CH_3COCH_3]^1[H^+]^1[I_2]^0$

Which one of the following statements is correct?
A The reaction is first order overall.
B The rate determining step cannot involve hydrogen ions.
C The rate determining step cannot involve iodine molecules.
D The yield of product is independent of the concentration of iodine.

2 For the reaction $H_2(g) + I_2(g) \rightarrow 2HI(g)$, the rate = $k[H_2(g)][I_2(g)]$. If the total pressure of the reaction mixture is doubled, the rate increases by
A 2×   B 4×   C 8×   D 16×

3 Which statement concerning homogeneous catalysts is **FALSE**?
A The catalyst and the reactants are all in the same physical state.
B The catalyst provides an alternative reaction path of lower activation energy.
C The catalyst improves the equilibrium yield of products.
D Homogeneous catalysts usually involve intermediate compound formation.

4 Which one of the following shows the units for the rate constant of a first order reaction?
A $dm\,mol^{-1}\,s^{-1}$ C $mol^2\,dm^{-6}\,s^{-1}$
B $mol\,dm^{-3}\,s^{-1}$ D s^{-1}

Grid question

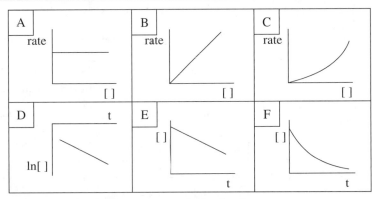

[ ] is the concentration of a reactant and t is the time.
Identify the graph(s) applying to:
(a) a second order reaction   (c) a zero order reaction
(b) the decay of a radioactive isotope

Multiple completion question

answer choice
A = (i)(ii)(iii)
B = (i)(iii)
C = (ii)(iv)
D = (iv)

Hydrochloric acid catalyses the hydrolysis of sucrose to a mixture of glucose and fructose: $C_{12}H_{22}O_{11} + H_2O \rightarrow 2C_6H_{12}O_6$. Which of the following could be measured to investigate the kinetics of the reaction?
(i) electrical conductivity
(ii) pH of the aqueous solution
(iii) intensity of colour of the reaction mixture
(iv) angle of rotation of plane polarized light

EXAMINATION QUESTIONS

Question 1

The following graph refers to the pressure of gaseous dinitrogen pentoxide, N_2O_5, during its decomposition at 65 °C.

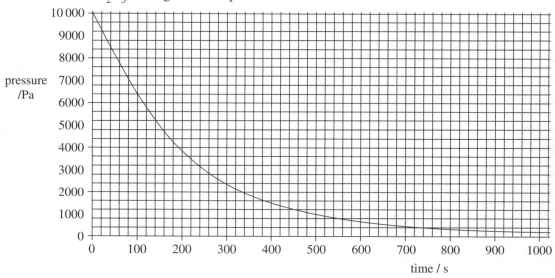

(a) (i) For initial pressures of 10 000 Pa, 6000 Pa and 4000 Pa determine the time to the nearest ten seconds for each pressure to halve.

10 000 Pa .... 6000 Pa .... 4000 Pa .... [3]

(ii) Use the above three answers to determine the order of the reaction, and explain your reasoning.

....

.... [2]

HINT
Have you still got your ruler?

(b) (i) What information would be given by the slope (gradient) of a tangent drawn to the curve at any point?

.... [1]

(ii) Sketch the graph you would expect to obtain if you plotted the negative slopes of the tangents to various points on the curve against the pressures of the dinitrogen pentoxide at those points.

−slope of
tangent

pressure of dinitrogen pentoxide

[2]

total 8 marks

Question 2

(a) The diagram below shows the distribution of molecular velocities in a given mass of gas at a particular temperature. The vertical axis is a function of the velocity.

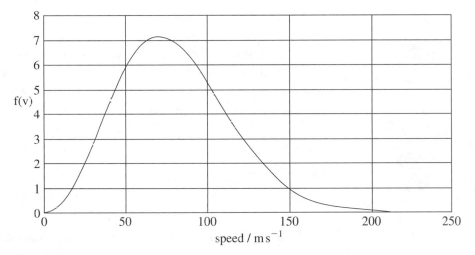

Draw on the grid a curve showing the distribution of molecular velocities
(i) at a lower temperature – label this curve **L**
(ii) at a higher temperature – label this curve **H**   [2]

(b) (i) What is meant by the term *activation energy*?

....

.... [1]

(ii) Sketch an energy profile for an exothermic reaction and mark on it the activation energy, E_a, for the forward reaction.   [2]

HINT
Don't turn a simple sketch into a work of art!

Energy

Reaction coordinate

(iii) On your sketch above, add and label a profile for the same reaction when it is catalysed.   [1]

(iv) Explain in terms of activation energy why the catalysed reaction proceeds at a greater rate.

....

....

....

.... [4]

total 10 marks

Question 3

At 700 K the decomposition of chloroethane $C_2H_5Cl(g) \rightarrow C_2H_4(g) + HCl(g)$ is a first order reaction. The decomposition can be followed by measuring the total pressure (p_t) of the system (at constant volume) at various times (t). A value for the rate constant k, can be determined by plotting $\ln\{a/(a-x)\}$ against t and measuring the gradient. a is the initial number of chloroethane molecules. x is the number of chloroethane molecules that have decomposed after a time t.

(a) When t = 0, the initial pressure, p_o, is proportional to the initial number of chloroethane molecules: $p_o \propto a$. Write similar expressions, using a and/or x, for the

  (i) partial pressure, p_e, of ethene in the system at time t

  .... [1]

  (ii) partial pressure, p_c, of chloroethane in the system at time t

  .... [1]

  (iii) total pressure, p_t, of the system at time t

  .... [1]

(b) (i) When $t = 0$, the initial number of chloroethane molecules may be related to the initial pressure by the expression: $a \propto p_o$. Using p_o and p_t, derive a similar expression for $a - x$.

  .... [2]

  (ii) Write an expression for $\ln\{a/(a-x)\}$ in terms of p_o and p_t.

  .... [1]

  (iii) Use the following data to plot a graph of $\ln\{a/(a-x)\}$ against time/min.

time/min	0	30	60	90	120	150	180
total pressure/kPa	100	107	114	121	126	132	136
$\ln\{a/(a-x)\}$							

HINT
Make the most of the graph paper.

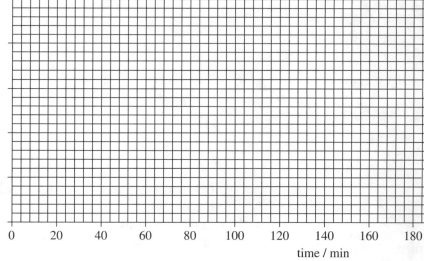

[4]

  (iv) From the gradient of the graph, determine a value for the rate constant k, for the decomposition of chloroethane at 700 K:

  .... [2]

total 12 marks

4 Chemical equilibria

Study Guide
Chapter 7

TOPIC OUTLINE

Dynamic equilibrium
Achieved when opposing kinetic molecular processes occur at exactly equal balancing rates so that the system's intensive properties (*pressure, concentration* and *temperature*) are constant.

Law of chemical equilibrium
If a reversible reaction aA + bB ⇌ cC + dD is at equilibrium *at a constant temperature*,

$$\frac{[C]^c \times [D]^d}{[A]^a \times [B]^b} = K_c \text{ or } \frac{P_C^c \times P_D^d}{P_A^a \times P_B^b} = K_p$$

[ ] represents concentration and *p* represents partial pressure.

Equilibrium constants (K_c and K_p)
Represent values that are constant when the concentrations and partial pressures in the above expressions are **equilibrium values**.

Units of K_c and K_p
Depend upon the equation for the reversible reaction. When (a+b) = (c+d), $K_c = K_p$ and the equilibrium constant (K) value has no units. If the equation for the reaction is written as cC + dD ⇌ aA + bB, the values for the equilibrium constants will be reciprocals of those for the previous constants K_c and K_p.

Equilibrium constant and temperature
▶ The value represented by K_c or K_p depends upon temperature.
If aA + bB ⇌ cC + dD (reading from left to right) is an *exothermic* reaction, then its *reverse reaction* (reading from right to left: i.e. cC + dD ⇌ aA + bB) is *endothermic*. With increasing temperature, the value of K_c or K_p increases for the endothermic direction and decreases for the exothermic direction.

The slope of a straight-line graph of ln K against $1/T$ gives a value for $-\Delta H^\ominus/R$.

Equilibrium constant and the system
▶ The value represented by K_c or K_p depends upon the chemical system.

Chemical System at 500 K	K_p	units	$\Delta H_{500}^\ominus$/kJ	$\Delta G_{500}^\ominus$/kJ
$H_2(g) + CO_2(g) \rightleftharpoons H_2O(g) + CO(g)$	7.8×10^{-3}	-	+41	+20
$N_2(g) + 3H_2(g) \rightleftharpoons 2NH_3(g)$	3.6×10^{-2}	atm^{-2}	-101	+14
$H_2(g) + I_2(g) \rightleftharpoons 2HI(g)$	25.0	-	-10	-13
$N_2O_4(g) \rightleftharpoons 2NO_2$	1.7×10^3	atm	+57	-30
$2SO_2(g) + O_2(g) \rightleftharpoons 2SO_3(g)$	2.5×10^{10}	atm^{-1}	-200	-90

Equilibrium constant and Gibbs free energy
▶ The standard free energy change, $\Delta G^\ominus = -RT \ln K$. So when $K > 1$, $\Delta G^\ominus$ is negative, the equilibrium favours products and the reaction is energetically feasible.
▶ If $\Delta G^\ominus$ is large and negative (< -60 kJ mol^{-1}) the reaction may be considered complete (insignificant amounts of reactants present in the equilibrium mixture).

► If $\Delta G^{\ominus}$ is large and positive ($> +60\,\mathrm{kJ\,mol^{-1}}$) the reaction may be considered not to take place (insignificant amounts of products in the equilibrium mixture).

Reference Guide for definitions

Equilibrium constant and concentration or partial pressure
The value represented by K_c or K_p is constant and independent of the concentrations ([ ]) and partial pressures (p).
For a given reversible reaction at equilibrium at a given temperature, if we add more substance (to increase a component's concentration or partial pressure) or we alter the volume of the system (to change the total pressure) we will **NOT** alter the constant value represented by K_c or K_p. We may, however, alter the composition of the mixture.
(See A-Level Chemisty Study Guide pp. 85–7 for further explanation.)

Equilibrium composition and total pressure
If total amount of gaseous reactants $>$ total amount of gaseous products, an increase in total pressure is accompanied by a shift in the composition in favour of products. If total amount of gaseous reactants $=$ total amount of gaseous products, a change in total pressure has no effect on the equilibrium composition.

Le Chatelier's principle
If the conditions of a reversible reaction are altered and disturb the equilibrium, the composition of the mixture may change to restore the equilibrium and to minimize the effect of altering the conditions.

Acid-base equilibria in water
► **Ionic product for water** (K_w)

$H_2O(l) + H_2O(l) \rightleftharpoons H_3O^+(aq) + OH^-(aq)$
$[H_2O(l)]$ approximately constant
$[H_3O^+(aq)] \times [OH^-(aq)] = K_w = 1 \times 10^{-14}\,\mathrm{mol^2\,dm^{-6}}$ at 298 K

► $\mathbf{p}K_w = -\log_{10}(K_w/\mathrm{mol^2\,dm^{-6}}) = 14$ at 298 K
For **pure water** $[H_3O^+(aq)] = [OH^-(aq)] = 1 \times 10^{-7}\,\mathrm{mol\,dm^{-3}}$ at 298 K.

► $\mathbf{pH} = -\log_{10}([H_3O^+(aq)]/\mathrm{mol\,dm^{-3}}) = 7$
► $\mathbf{pOH} = -\log_{10}([OH^-(aq)]/\mathrm{mol\,dm^{-3}}) = 7$
► $\mathbf{p}K_w = \mathbf{pH} + \mathbf{pOH} = 14$

pH scale of acidity

$[H_3O^+(aq)]$ /$\mathrm{mol\,dm^{-3}}$ $\longrightarrow$ 10^{-1} $\qquad$ 10^{-7} $\qquad$ 10^{-13}

pH 1 2 3 4 5 6 7 8 9 10 11 12 13

acidic $\quad$ neutral $\quad$ alkaline
$[H^+] > [OH^-]$ $\quad$ $[H^+] = [OH^-]$ $\quad$ $[H^+] < [OH^-]$

13 12 11 10 9 8 7 6 5 4 3 2 1 pOH

10^{-13} $\qquad$ 10^{-7} $\qquad$ 10^{-1} $\longleftarrow$ $[OH^-(aq)]$ /$\mathrm{mol\,dm^{-3}}$

Strong acids and bases
► For **strong acid** $0.1\,\mathrm{mol\,dm^{-3}}$ HCl(aq),
$[H_3O^+(aq)] = 0.1$ so pH $= 1$ and pOH $= 13$
► For **strong base** $0.1\,\mathrm{mol\,dm^{-3}}$ NaOH(aq),
$[OH^-(aq)] = 0.1$ so pOH $= 1$ and pH $= 13$
► Strong acids, strong bases and salts are *completely ionized* in water.

Weak acids and bases

▶ *Weak acids* (HA) only *partially ionize* in water into their conjugate bases (A^-).

$$CH_3CO_2H(aq) + H_2O(l) \rightleftharpoons H_3O^+(aq) + CH_3CO_2^-(aq)$$

$$\frac{[H_3O^+(aq)][CH_3CO_2^-(aq)]}{[CH_3CO_2H(aq)]} = K_a$$

▶ *Weak bases* (BOH) only *partially ionize* in water into their conjugate acids (B^+).

$$NH_3(aq) + H_2O(l) \rightleftharpoons NH_4^+(aq) + OH^-(aq)$$

$$\frac{[NH_4^+(aq)][OH^-(aq)]}{[NH_3(aq)]} = K_b$$

Dissociation constants

K_a is the acid dissociation constant and K_b is the base dissociation constant. When the proton donor (e.g. NH_4^+) and proton acceptor (e.g. NH_3) are acid and conjugate base, then $K_a \times K_b = K_w$ and $pK_a + pK_b = pK_w = 14$.

Simplifying assumptions

Weak acids (or bases) may often be regarded as unionized when calculating the concentration [HA] (or [BOH]) of their molecules. At the same time the weak acid (or base) may often be considered to supply all the $H_3O^+(aq)$ ions (or $OH^-(aq)$ ions) so that $[H_3O^+(aq)] = [A^-(aq)]$ (or $[OH^-(aq)] = [B^+(aq)]$).

Acid–base indicators

Weak acids or bases whose aqueous acid is a different colour from its aqueous conjugate base. An indicator solution shows its *mid-point colour* when $[HInd] = [Ind^-]$ and the pH = pK_{ind}.

Buffers

▶ Solutions of a given pH which resist changes to that pH when contaminated with small amounts of acid or alkali. *N.B.* There is a change to the pH, but if the amount of acid or alkali is small, the change has no practical significance.

▶ A buffer solution contains an aqueous weak acid and its conjugate base (or an aqueous weak base and its conjugate acid) often in equal concentration to give its *maximum buffering effect*, so [HA] = [A^-] and the pH of the buffer = pK_a. In general,

$$pH_{buffer} = pK_a + \log_{10}([\text{conjugate base}]/[\text{weak acid}]).$$

$$pOH_{buffer} = pK_b + \log_{10}([\text{conjugate acid}]/[\text{weak base}]).$$

▶ For a buffer solution made from a weak acid and one of its salts:

$$pH_{buffer} = pK_a + \log_{10}([\text{salt}]/[\text{weak acid}]).$$

▶ For a buffer solution made from a weak base and one of its salts:

$$pOH_{buffer} = pK_b + \log_{10}([\text{salt}]/[\text{weak base}]).$$

▶ If a buffer is diluted with water, the pH (or pOH) does not change because the ratio [salt]/[weak acid] (or [salt]/[weak base]) does not change.

★ REVISION ACTIVITY

Multiple choice questions

1 Which one of the following can increase the equilibrium yield of sulphur trioxide in the reaction $2SO_2(g) + O_2(g) \rightleftharpoons 2SO_3(g); \Delta H = -197\,kJ\,mol^{-1}$?
   A decreasing the total pressure   C increasing the partial pressure of oxygen
   B increasing the temperature   D using a vanadium pentoxide catalyst

2 Which one of the following represents
   K_p for $2H_2(g) + CO(g) \rightleftharpoons CH_3OH(g)$?

   A $p_{H_2} \times p_{CO}/p_{CH_3OH}$

   B $p_{CH_3OH}/p_{H_2} \times p_{CO}$

   C $p_{H_2}^2 \times p_{CO}/p_{CH_3OH}$

   D $p_{CH_3OH}/p_{H_2}^2 \times p_{CO}$

3 Which one of the following shows the units of
   K_c for $N_2(g) + 3H_2(g) \rightleftharpoons 2NH_3(g)$?
   A $mol\,dm^{-3}$ B $dm^3\,mol^{-1}$ C $mol^2\,dm^{-6}$ D $dm^6\,mol^{-2}$

4 Which one of the following expressions is **INCORRECT**?
   A $pK_a = pK_w/pK_b$ C $pH = -\log([H^+]/mol\,dm^{-3})$
   B $pK_a = -\log(K_a/mol\,dm^{-3})$ D $pOH = -\log([OH^-]/mol\,dm^{-3})$

5 Which one of the following acid and conjugate base pairs would make an acidic buffer?
   A NH_4^+/NH_3 C HCO_3^-/CO_3^{2-}
   B $CH_3CO_2H/CH_3CO_2^-$ D HPO_4^{2-}/PO_4^{3-}

Grid question

A	titrate hydrochloric acid into sodium hydroxide	B	titrate hydrochloric acid into aqueous ammonia	C	titrate ethanoic acid into sodium hydroxide
D	methyl orange $pK_{ind} = 3.5$	E	bromothymol blue $pK_{ind} = 7.0$	F	phenolphthalein $pK_{ind} = 9.3$

Identify the titration of:
(a) a strong acid into a strong base and the one most suitable indicator
(b) a weak acid into a strong base and the one most suitable indicator
(c) a strong acid into a weak base and the one most suitable indicator

Multiple completion question

answer choice
A = (i)(ii)(iii)
B = (i)(iii)
C = (ii)(iv)
D = (iv)

Which of the following can act as both a Lewis acid and a Lewis base?
   (i) HCO_3^-
   (ii) $[Cu(H_2O)_6]^{2+}$
   (iii) HPO_4^{2-}
   (iv) $[Cu(NH_3)_4(H_2O)_2]^{2+}$

EXAMINATION QUESTIONS

Question 1

(a) (i) Write down an expression for K_c for the each of the following:

reaction A $2SO_2(g) + O_2(g) \rightleftharpoons 2SO_3(g)$; $\Delta H^\ominus = -197 \, kJ \, mol^{-1}$

HINT
Never leave this kind of question [(a)(ii)] unanswered.

reaction B $H_2(g) + I_2(g) \rightleftharpoons 2HI(g)$; $\Delta H^\ominus = -9.6 \, kJ \, mol^{-1}$

[2]

(ii) For which of the two reactions, at any given temperature, will the value of

K_p equal the value of K_c?.. [1]

(b) State the effect of each of the following on the equilibrium amount of sulphur trioxide in **reaction A**.

(i) increasing the total pressure on the system

....

(ii) increasing the temperature of the system

....

(iii) adding a catalyst

....

(iv) increasing the partial pressure of the oxygen

.... [4]

(d) The reaction $N_2(g) + 3H_2(g) \rightleftharpoons 2NH_3(g)$; $\Delta H^\ominus = -92 \, kJ \, mol^{-1}$ plays a crucial part in a major industrial process.

(i) Give the name of the industrial process.

.... [1]

(ii) Give the name and type of catalyst used in the process.

.... [2]

(iii) State **two** important uses of the product of this process.

....

.... [2]

total 12 marks

Question 2
(a) Define pH

.... [1]

(b) Calculate the pH of
   (i) hydrochloric acid of concentration $0.1 \, mol \, dm^{-3}$

.... [1]

   (ii) aqueous ethanoic acid of concentration $0.1 \, mol \, dm^{-3}$
        (K_a for ethanoic acid is $1.8 \times 10^{-5} \, mol \, dm^{-3}$)

....

....

.... [2]

   (iii) aqueous ammonia of concentration $0.1 \, mol \, dm^{-3}$
         (pK_a for the ammonium ion is 9.25 and pK_w is 14)

....

....

.... [2]

HINT

Could simplifications avoid a quadratic?

(c) The diagram below shows the changes in pH when aqueous sodium hydroxide of concentration $0.1 \, mol \, dm^{-3}$ is added separately to $25 \, cm^3$ of hydrochloric acid and $25 \, cm^3$ of ethanoic acid. Each aqueous acid has a concentration of $0.1 \, mol \, dm^{-3}$.

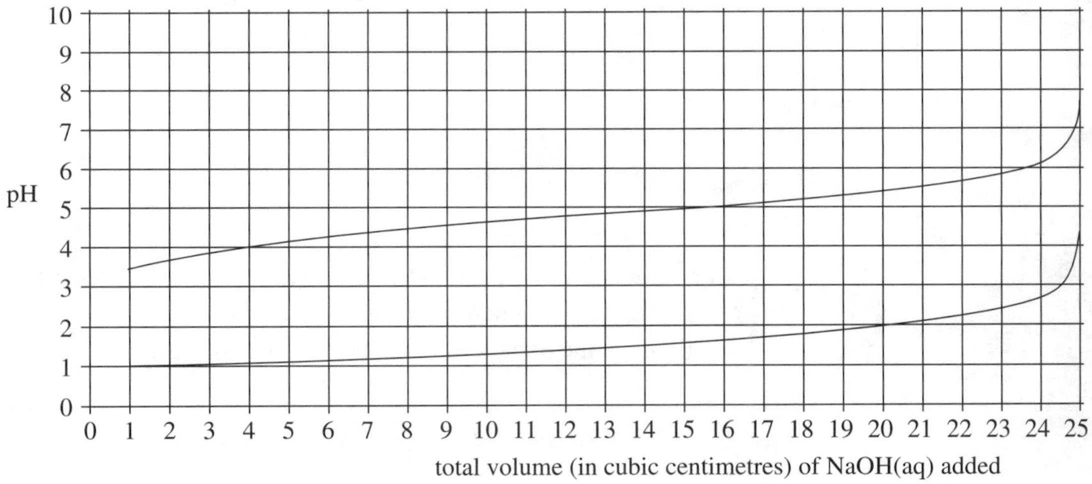

total volume (in cubic centimetres) of NaOH(aq) added

   (i) Explain why methyl orange (pH range 3.1 to 4.4) is a suitable indicator when titrating aqueous sodium hydroxide into one of the acids but not into the other.

....

....

.... [2]

   (ii) What type of solution is formed by adding $12.5 \, cm^3$ of the alkali to the $25 \, cm^3$ of the ethanoic acid and what is the significance of its pH value?

....

.... [2]

total 10 marks

Question 3

(a) Many acid–base indicators are weak acids whose aqueous solution has a different colour from that of its conjugate base. The dissociation of the indicator molecules (HInd) into their conjugate bases (Ind^-) may be represented by

$$HInd(aq) \rightleftharpoons H^+(aq) + Ind^-(aq)$$
colour 1   colour 2

The pH range of such indicators is approximately $pK_{ind} \pm 1$.

(i) Show that $pH = pK_{ind} + \log [Ind^-(aq)]/[HInd(aq)]$

....

....

....

....

....

.... [3]

(ii) If HInd(aq) is yellow, Ind^-(aq) is blue and pK_{ind} is 4.0, what is the pH of the indicator solution whose colour is green (the mid-point colour of the indicator)?

.... [1]

(iii) If HInd(aq) is yellow, Ind^-(aq) is blue and pK_{ind} is 7.0, state and explain what colour would be formed on adding the indicator to $0.1 \, mol \, dm^{-3}$ NaOH(aq)?

....

.... [2]

(b) (i) State what is meant by the term *buffer solution*.

....

....

.... [2]

(ii) Explain how an aqueous solution containing ethanoic acid and sodium ethanoate behaves as a buffer solution.

....

....

....

....

....

.... [4]

(iii) Calculate the pH of a buffer solution containing $0.10 \, mol \, dm^{-3}$ of ethanoic acid and $0.40 \, mol \, dm^{-3}$ of sodium ethanoate.
(The value of K_a for ethanoic acid is $1.8 \times 10^{-5} \, mol \, dm^{-3}$)

....

....

....

.... [4]

total 16 marks

HINT
Count the lines and watch your time.

5 Electrochemistry and redox

Study Guide
Chapter 8

Oxidation
Increase in
oxidation number.
Reduction
Decrease in
oxidation number.

● TOPIC OUTLINE

Oxidation and reduction
▶ **Reduction** Loss of oxygen, gain of hydrogen or gain of electrons by the oxidant.
▶ **Oxidation** Gain of oxygen, loss of hydrogen or loss of electrons by the reductant.
▶ **Redox** Transfer of electrons from reductant to oxidant.

Oxidation numbers
Range from -4 to $+7$ and may be assigned to every element by
the following set of rules *applied in priority order*:

1	oxidation number of an uncombined element	0
2	sum of oxidation numbers of elements in uncharged formula	0
3	sum of oxidation numbers of elements in charged formula	charge
4	oxidation number of fluorine in any formula	-1
5	oxidation number of an alkali metal in any formula	$+1$
6	oxidation number of an alkaline earth metal in any formula	$+2$
7	oxidation number of oxygen (except in peroxides $= -1$)	-2
8	oxidation number of halogen in metal halides	-1
9	oxidation number of hydrogen (except in metal hydrides $= -1$)	$+1$

Metal displacement
Redox in which metal (reductant) is oxidized by loss of electrons and cation
(oxidant) is reduced by gain of electrons: e.g.

$$Zn(s) + 2H^+(aq) \rightarrow Zn^{2+}(aq) + H_2(g)$$

Non-metal displacement
Redox in which non-metal (oxidant) is reduced by gain of electrons and anion
(reductant) is oxidized by loss of electrons: e.g.

$$Cl_2(g) + 2Br^-(aq) \rightarrow 2Cl^-(aq) + Br_2(aq)$$

Disproportionation
Redox in which the oxidation number of the same element in a reactant simulta-
neously increases and decreases: e.g. $Cl_2(0)$ to $Cl^-(-1) + ClO^-(+1)$
in the reaction $Cl_2(g) + 2OH^-(aq) \rightarrow Cl^-(aq) + ClO^-(aq) + H_2O(l)$.

Electromotive force (E)
Maximum potential difference (voltage) between the electrodes of an electrochemical cell. The e.m.f. is the potential difference when the cell is giving no
current, so the e.m.f. can only be measured using a potentiometer or very high
resistance voltmeter.

Standard e.m.f. $(E^\ominus)$
Maximum voltage of an electrochemical cell under standard conditions; i.e. temperature 25 °C (298 K), pressure 1 atm (101 kPa) and solutions of concentration
1 mol dm^{-3} (unit activity).

Standard electrode potential ($E^\ominus$)

Defined as the e.m.f. of an electrochemical cell represented by a cell diagram in which a standard hydrogen electrode is shown as the left-hand half-cell. This defines as zero the standard electrode potential of the hydrogen electrode.
Pt [H_2(g)] | $2H^+$(aq) $\vdots$ Zn^{2+}(aq) | Zn(s); $E^\ominus = -0.76$ V.

Apparatus diagrams and cell diagrams

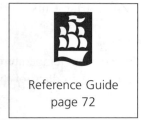
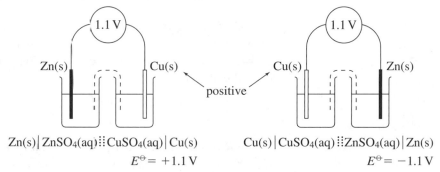

$Zn(s) | ZnSO_4(aq) \vdots CuSO_4(aq) | Cu(s)$ $Cu(s) | CuSO_4(aq) \vdots ZnSO_4(aq) | Zn(s)$
$E^\ominus = +1.1$ V $E^\ominus = -1.1$ V

In **cell diagrams** e.m.f. is given sign of right-hand electrode.

Standard hydrogen electrode

Half-cell consisting of pure hydrogen gas, at 25 °C and 1 atm pressure, bubbling past a platinized platinum electrode dipping into a 1 mol dm^{-3} solution of H_3O^+(aq).

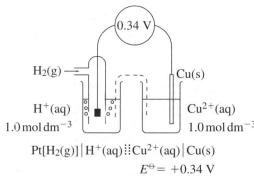

$Pt[H_2(g)] | H^+(aq) \vdots Cu^{2+}(aq) | Cu(s)$
$E^\ominus = +0.34$ V

Combining half-cells

▶ Any two half-cells may be combined to produce a complete electrochemical cell.

I_2(aq), $2I^-$(aq) | Pt $E^\ominus = +0.54$ V

Fe^{3+}(aq), Fe^{2+}(aq) | Pt $E^\ominus = +0.77$ V

Pt | $2I^-$(aq), I_2(aq) $\vdots$ Fe^{3+}(aq), Fe^{2+}(aq) | Pt

▶ The standard e.m.f may be found from the standard electrode potentials of the two half-cells:

$E_{cell} = E_{\text{right-hand half-cell}} - E_{\text{left-hand half-cell}}$

$= (+0.77) - (+0.54)$

hence Pt | $2I^-$(aq), I_2(aq) $\vdots$ Fe^{3+}(aq), Fe^{2+}(aq) | Pt $E^\ominus = +0.23$ V

or Pt | Fe^{2+}(aq), Fe^{3+}(aq) $\vdots$ I_2(aq), $2I^-$(aq) | Pt $E^\ominus = -0.23$ V

Cell reactions

A spontaneous redox reaction occurs when an electrochemical cell is short-circuited by connecting together by a wire the metal electrodes of the two half-cells. Electrons travel in the wire from the negative half-cell (where oxidation is occurring) to the positive half-cell (where reduction is occurring). For example, in the Daniell cell, electrons travel from the zinc to the copper electrode.

The Daniell cell

► **cell diagram** $Zn(s) \mid Zn^{2+}(aq) \vdots Cu^{2+}(aq) \mid Cu(s)$

► **l.h.half-cell reaction** $Zn(s) \rightarrow Zn^{2+}(aq) + 2e^-$

► **r.h.half-cell reaction** $Cu^{2+}(aq) + 2e^- \rightarrow Cu(s)$

► **overall spontaneous cell reaction** $Zn(s) + Cu^{2+}(aq) \rightarrow Zn^{2+}(aq) + Cu(s)$

The Nernst equation

Shows how the e.m.f. (E_{cell}) of an electrochemical cell at a constant temperature T (= 298 K) depends upon the concentrations of the reactant and products of the overall cell reaction

$$E_{cell} = E_{cell}^{\ominus} + \frac{RT}{zF} \ln \frac{[Cu^{2+}(aq)]}{[Zn^{2+}(aq)]}$$

where R is the Gas constant ($8.31\,J\,K^{-1}\,mol^{-1}$), T is the standard temperature (298 K), F is the Faraday constant ($96\,500\,C\,mol^{-1}$) and z is the number of moles of electrons transferred per mole of redox reaction. (This is specified by the equation for the cell reaction whose equilibrium constant value is represented by K_c). *N.B.* The standard e.m.f. ($E_{cell}^{\ominus}$) of the electrochemical cell refers to the same constant temperature T (= 298 K), so the Nernst equation **cannot** be used to calculate e.m.f. values at different temperatures.

Standard cell e.m.f. and equilibrium

When the e.m.f. of a short-circuited electrochemical cell falls to zero (flat battery), the overall cell reaction achieves equilibrium. Hence, $E_{cell}^{\ominus} = (RT/zF)\ln K_c$

Free energy change, e.m.f. and equilibrium constants

$\Delta G^{\ominus} = -RT \ln K_c$ and $\Delta G^{\ominus} = -zFE^{\ominus}$

For the Daniell cell, $E^{\ominus} = 1.10\,V$ so $\Delta G^{\ominus}$ is $-2 \times 96\,500 \times 1.10 = -212\,300$ $J\,mol^{-1}$. Therefore $-\ln K_c$ is $-212\,300/(8.31 \times 298) = -85.7$ and hence $K_c = 1.71 \times 10^{37}$. The very large negative value for $\Delta G^{\ominus}$ and the very large positive value for K_c show that for all practical purposes the reaction is complete. Thus excess zinc metal added to aqueous copper(II) sulphate would be expected to displace all the copper.

Study Guide
pages 75–6

Energetic feasibility of redox reactions

Standard potentials may be used to *predict* the feasibility of redox reactions. The following reduction potentials indicate that it is energetically feasible for bromine to displace iodine from aqueous potassium iodide but that it is not energetically feasible for bromine to displace chlorine from aqueous potassium chloride.

$I_2(aq) + 2e^- \rightarrow 2I^-(aq)$ $E^{\ominus} = +0.54\,V$

$Br_2(aq) + 2e^- \rightarrow 2Br^-(aq)$ $E^{\ominus} = +1.09\,V$
                              $Br_2(aq) + 2I^-(aq) \rightarrow 2Br^-(aq) + I_2(aq)$

$Cl_2(aq) + 2e^- \rightarrow 2Cl^-(aq)$ $E^{\ominus} = +1.36\,V$
                              $Cl_2(aq) + 2Br^-(aq) \rightarrow 2Cl^-(aq) + Br_2(aq)$

Energetically feasible redox reactions always will occur spontaneously within an electrochemical cell when it is short-circuited. The same reactions may not take place when the reductants and oxidants are put directly in contact with one another in a test tube. The direct contact reactions may take place slowly or not at all if they are kinetically hindered and therefore have high activation energies.

★ REVISION ACTIVITY

Multiple choice questions

1 In which one of the following does the metal, M, have its highest oxidation number?

  A MO_4^-(aq)   **B** MCl_4^{2-}(aq)   **C** MO^{2+}(aq)   **D** M_2O^+(aq)

2 Which one of the following is **NOT** a disproportionation reaction?

  A $Cl_2 + 2NaOH \rightarrow NaCl + NaClO + H_2O$

  B $3K_2MnO_4 + 2H_2O \rightarrow 2KMnO_4 + MnO_2 + 4KOH$

  C $2K_2CrO_4 + H_2SO_4 \rightarrow K_2Cr_2O_7 + K_2SO_4 + H_2O$

  D $N_2O_4 + 2NaOH \rightarrow NaNO_3 + NaNO_2$

3 The standard reduction potential of Al^{3+}(aq) $\rightarrow$ Al(s) + 3e$^-$ is -1.66 V and the standard reduction potential of Cu^{2+}(aq) $\rightarrow$ Cu(s) + 2e$^-$ is $+0.34$ V. Which one of the following is the standard e.m.f. of the cell Al(s) | Al^{3+}(aq) ⋮ Cu^{2+}(aq)|Cu(s)?

  A $+2.00$ V   **B** -2.00 V   **C** $+1.32$ V   **D** -1.32 V

4 Which one of the following would **NOT** oxidize I$^-$(aq) to I_2(aq)?

  A Fe^{3+}(aq)   **B** $Cr_2O_7^{2-}$(aq)   **C** MnO_4^-(aq)   **D** $S_2O_3^{2-}$(aq)

5 10 cm^3 of hot aqueous potassium manganate(VII) of concentration 0.1 mol dm^{-3} quantitatively oxidizes 25 cm^3 of aqueous ethanedioic acid according to the equation

$$MnO_4^-(aq) + 3H^+(aq) + 2\tfrac{1}{2}(CO_2H)_2(aq) \rightarrow Mn^{2+}(aq) + 4H_2O(l) + 5CO_2(g).$$

What is the concentration of the ethanedioic acid in mol dm^{-3}?

  A 0.25   **B** 0.1   **C** 0.0625   **D** 0.04

Grid question

The grid shows the possible effects of short-circuiting a standard cell using a wire. The standard cell is M(s)|M^{m+}(aq) ⋮ X_2(aq), $2X^-$(aq)|Pt. The standard reduction potentials, in volts, for Zn^{2+}, Ag^+, I_2 and Cl_2 are -0.76, $+0.80$, $+0.54$ and $+1.36$ respectively.

A	B	C
metal atoms M oxidize to metal ions M^{m+}	electrons flow from the platinum to the metal M	halogen molecules X_2 reduce to halide ions X^-
D	**E**	**F**
metal ions M^{m+} reduce to metal atoms M	electrons flow from the metal M to the platinum	halide ions X^- oxidize to halogen molecules X_2

Identify the effects of short-circuiting the cell when
(a) the metal M is zinc, Zn, and the halogen X is chlorine, Cl
(b) the metal M is silver, Ag, and the halogen X is iodine, I

Multiple completion question

answer choice
A = (i)(ii)(iii)
B = (i)(iii)
C = (ii)(iv)
D = (iv)

In which of the following would the transition metal have an oxidation state of +2?

  (i) $CuCl_2^-$ (iii) $[Fe(H_2O)_5OH]^{2+}$

  (ii) $CoCl_4^{2-}$ (iv) $[Cu(NH_3)_4(H_2O)_2]^{2+}$

EXAMINATION QUESTIONS

Question 1

(a) The diagram on the right shows a standard hydrogen electrode.

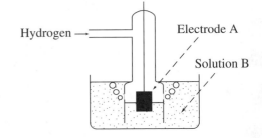

   (i) State the pressure of the hydrogen gas.

   .... [1]

   (ii) Describe briefly the nature of electrode A.

.... [1]

   (iii) State the composition and concentration of solution B.

.... [2]

(b) The electrode potential of a metal half-cell, under non-standard conditions, is given by the Nernst equation:

$$E = E^{\ominus} + \frac{RT}{nF} \ln[\text{oxidized form}]$$

where R is the gas constant, T is the temperature in Kelvin, F is the Faraday constant, n is the number of electrons involved in the half-reaction and [oxidised form] is the concentration of the metal ion in mol dm^{-3}.

A series of silver half-cells, $Ag^+(aq) + e^- \rightleftharpoons Ag(s)$, were set up at 298 K. The concentration of the aqueous silver ions was varied and the e.m.f. of each cell was measured against the standard hydrogen electrode. The results are shown below.

<table>
<tr><td>

HINT

Do you know the mathematical equation for a straight line?

</td></tr>
</table>

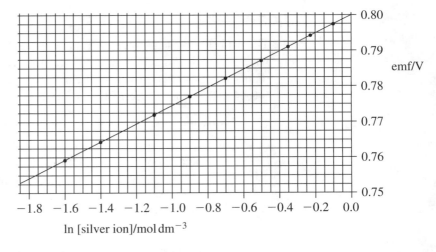

ln [silver ion]/mol dm^{-3}

   (i) What is the standard electrode potential of silver?

.... [1]

   (ii) What concentration of silver ions would give an e.m.f. of 0.78 volts?

.... [2]

   (iii) Derive an approximate value for the Faraday constant.
        ($R = 8.3 \, \text{J K}^{-1}\text{mol}^{-1}$)

....

.... [2]

total 9 marks

Question 2

(a) Define the term *standard electrode potential* as applied to a metallic element.

....

.... [2]

(b) The standard electrode potentials, $E^{\ominus}$, of zinc and copper are $-0.76\,\text{V}$ and $+0.34\,\text{V}$ respectively.

   (i) Draw an apparatus diagram to show a standard cell in which zinc is in contact with aqueous zinc sulphate in a beaker and copper in contact with aqueous copper(II) sulphate in a similar beaker.

HINT
Don't confuse a cell diagram with diagram of a cell.

                                                      [2]

   (ii) What is the e.m.f. of this cell? ....volts. [1]

   (iii) What instrument would be used to measure this e.m.f?

.... [1]

   (iv) In which direction would electrons flow in a wire used to connect together the copper and zinc electrodes?

.... [1]

   (v) Write an equation for the overall spontaneous cell reaction which would occur when the copper and zinc electrodes are connected together by a wire.

.... [1]

(c) The table below shows standard redox potentials of selected reductions.

ion/electron half-equation	$E^{\ominus}/\text{V}$
$BrO_3^- + 6H^+ + 5e^- \rightleftharpoons \frac{1}{2}Br_2 + 3H_2O$	$+1.52$
$\frac{1}{2}I_2 + e^- \rightleftharpoons I^-$	$+0.54$
$Fe^{3+} + e^- \rightleftharpoons Fe^{2+}$	$+0.77$
$Ag^+ + e^- \rightleftharpoons Ag$	$+0.80$

Predict, giving reasons, what reaction (if any) could occur in **each** of the following.

(i) Aqueous potassium iodide is added to acidified potassium bromate(V).

....

.... [2]

(ii) Metallic silver is added to aqueous iron(III) sulphate.

....

.... [2]

(iii) Aqueous iron(III) chloride and aqueous potassium iodide are mixed.

....

.... [2]

total 14 marks

Question 3

Vanadium is a transition element which can exist in oxidation states of 0, +2, +3, +4 and +5. The standard redox potentials for vanadium compounds in acidic solution are shown in the following table.

HINT

Can you work out oxidation numbers?

Reaction	$E^{\ominus}$/ V
$VO_2^+(aq) + 2H^+(aq) + e^- \rightleftharpoons VO^{2+}(aq) + H_2O(l)$	+1.00
$VO^{2+}(aq) + 2H^+(aq) + e^- \rightleftharpoons V^{3+}(aq) + H_2O(l)$	+0.34
$V^{3+}(aq) + e^- \rightleftharpoons V^{2+}(aq)$	−0.26

(a) Which of the vanadium ions shown in the table would be expected to be the strongest reducing agent? Give a reason for your answer.

....

.... [2]

(b) The standard redox potential of iodine $I_2(aq) + 2e^- \rightleftharpoons 2I^-(aq)$ is +0.54 V. Which of the vanadium ions shown in the table would be expected to oxidize aqueous iodide ions in acidic solution? Give reasons for your answer.

....

....

.... [3]

(c) The standard redox potential of zinc $Zn^{2+}(aq) + 2e^- \rightleftharpoons Zn(s)$ is −0.76 V. What would be the effect of treating vanadium(V) sulphate in acidic solution with excess zinc? Give a reason for your answer.

....

....

....

.... [3]

(d) The standard redox potential of aqueous sulphur dioxide

$$SO_4^{2-}(aq) + 4H^+(aq) + 2e^- \rightleftharpoons H_2SO_3(aq) + H_2O(l) \text{ is } +0.17 \text{ V.}$$

What would be expected to occur when vanadium(V) sulphate in acidic solution is treated with sodium sulphite? Give reasons for your answer.

....

....

....

.... [3]

total 11 marks

6 The Periodic Table

The Periodic Table

Elements are arranged in atomic number order.

													H 1	He 2							

s-block / p-block / d-block / f-block

s-block												p-block					
Li 3	Be 4											B 5	C 6	N 7	O 8	F 9	Ne 10
Na 11	Mg 12				d-block							Al 13	Si 14	P 15	S 16	Cl 17	Ar 18
K 19	Ca 20	Sc 21	Ti 22	V 23	Cr 24	Mn 25	Fe 26	Co 27	Ni 28	Cu 29	Zn 30	Ga 31	Ge 32	As 33	Se 34	Br 35	Kr 36
Rb 37	Sr 38	Y 39	Zr 40	Nb 41	Mo 42	Tc 43	Ru 44	Rh 45	Pd 46	Ag 47	Cd 48	In 49	Sn 50	Sb 51	Te 52	I 53	Xe 54
Cs 55	Ba 56	La 57	Hf 72	Ta 73	W 74	Re 75	Os 76	Ir 77	Pt 78	Au 79	Hg 80	Tl 81	Pb 82	Bi 83	Po 84	At 85	Rn 86
Fr 87	Ra 88	Ac 89															

f-block

Ce 58	Pr 59	Nd 60	Pm 61	Sm 62	Eu 63	Gd 64	Tb 65	Dy 66	Ho 67	Er 68	Tm 69	Yb 70	Lu 71
Th 90	Pa 91	U 92	Np 93	Pu 94	Am 95	Cm 96	Bk 97	Cf 98	Es 99	Fm 100	Md 101	No 102	Lr 103

Study Guide
Chapter 10

▶ **Period** *Horizontal row* of elements.
▶ **Group** *Vertical column* of elements.
▶ **Blocks** s-, p-, d- and f-blocks. Elements are arranged in increasing atomic number into *four blocks*.
  – The s- and p-blocks are *divided vertically into groups*.
  – The d- and f-block elements are *divided horizontally into rows*.

Periodicity

The recurrence of similar properties *at regular intervals* when elements are arranged in increasing atomic number order.

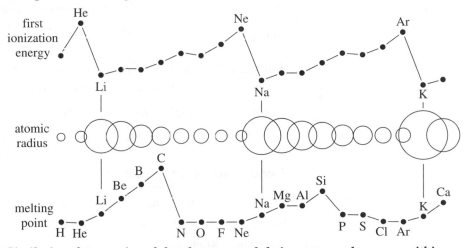

Similarity of properties of the elements and their compounds occurs within each group of the s- and p-blocks.

Atypical properties

Each of the elements in the first period (Li to F) have some properties that are **not** typical of their group.

Group 1 (alkali metals)	Group 4	Group 7 (halogens)
$Li_2CO_3 \rightarrow Li_2O + CO_2$ other alkali metal carbonates do not decompose in test tube	tetrachloromethane does not readily hydrolyse in test tube $SiCl_4 + 2H_2O \rightarrow SiO_2 + 4HCl$	Silver fluoride water soluble but other silver halides are not $Ag^+(aq) + Cl^-(aq) \rightarrow AgCl(s)$

This *atypical* behaviour of the first element in each group may be related to the
► very small atom size
► very high polarizing power of the cation
► very low polarizability of the anion
► high electronegativity
► inability of the 2nd shell to extend the number of its electrons beyond eight.

Study Guide
Chapters 11 and 12

Patterns and trends

The Periodic Table shows important patterns and trends in the properties of elements and their compounds.

From **left to right across the s- and p-block** elements:
► Atomic and ionic radius *decrease*.
► Tendency of chlorides to hydrolyse *increases*.

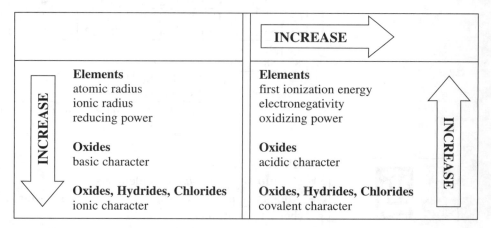

Basic elements (metals)

Form only cations and their (hydr)oxides react with acids but not alkalis:

$$MgO(s) + 2H^+(aq) \rightarrow Mg^{2+}(aq) + H_2O(l).$$

Acidic elements (non-metals)

Form only anions and their (hydr)oxides react with alkalis but not acids:

$$CO_2(g) + 2OH^-(aq) \rightarrow CO_3^{2-}(aq) + H_2O(l).$$

Amphoteric elements (metals or metalloids)

Form cations and anions and their (hydr)oxides react with acids and alkalis:

$$Al_2O_3(s) + 6H^+(aq) \rightarrow 2Al^{3+}(aq) + 3H_2O(l)$$

and $Al_2O_3(s) + 6OH^-(aq) + 3H_2O(l) \rightarrow 2[Al(OH)_6]^{3-}(aq).$

Trend in acid–base character

As oxidation number increases	+2 basic	+3 amphoteric	+6 acidic
basic character decreases and	Fe^{2+} Cr^{2+}	Fe^{3+} Cr^{3+}	FeO_4^{2-} CrO_4^{2-}
acidic character increases		FeO_2^- $[Cr(OH)_6]^{3-}$	$Cr_2O_7^{2-}$

Study Guide
Chapter 13

Similarity of properties of the elements and their compounds occurs within the rows of the d-block (transition metals) and f-block (lanthanides and actinides). Characteristic physical and chemical properties of transition metals (Ti–Cu) may be related to their *incomplete 3d-subshell* and *variable oxidation states.*

oxidation numbers (oxidation numbers in boxes refer to the most stable oxidation states) — **electronic configurations**

Oxidation no.	Sc	Ti	V	Cr	Mn	Fe	Co	Ni	Cu	Zn
7					[7]					
6				[6]	6	6				
5			[5]	5	5	5	5			
4		[4]	4	4	[4]	4	4	4		
3	[3]	3	3	[3]	3	[3]	[3]	3	3	
2		2	2	2	[2]	[2]	[2]	[2]	2	[2]
1	1	1	1	1	1	1	1	[1]		

Electronic configurations (orbital box diagrams, 4s above 3d):

	Sc	Ti	V	Cr	Mn	Fe	Co	Ni	Cu	Zn
4s	↑↓	↑↓	↑↓	↑	↑↓	↑↓	↑↓	↑↓	↑	↑↓
3d				↑	↑	↑	↑	↑	↑↓	↑↓
3d				↑	↑	↑	↑	↑	↑↓	↑↓
3d			↑	↑	↑	↑	↑	↑↓	↑↓	↑↓
3d		↑	↑	↑	↑	↑	↑↓	↑↓	↑↓	↑↓
3d	↑	↑	↑	↑	↑	↑↓	↑↓	↑↓	↑↓	↑↓

oxidation numbers in boxes refer to the most stable oxidation states

Transition metals
- ► hard, paramagnetic solids
- ► high m.pt. and b.pt.
- ► act as heterogeneous catalysts
- ► readily form alloys and interstitial compounds.

Transition metal ions
- ► form complex compounds
- ► act as homogeneous catalysts
- ► form highly coloured aqueous solutions
- ► show variable oxidation number of the element

Complex ions
Central metal cation with six (four or two) ligands (molecules or ions) datively bonded to it.
- ► *ligand* Atom (or small group of atoms) datively bonded by a lone electron-pair to a central transition metal cation.
- ► *monodentate* (one tooth) ligand forms one dative bond.
  - – molecules CO, H_2O, NH_3
  - – ions OH^-, CN^-, F^-, Cl^-
- ► *bidentate* (two teeth) ligand consists of several atoms, two of which are each capable of forming one dative bond with the central ion.
  - – molecule $NH_2CH_2CH_2NH_2$
  - – ion $^-O_2C.CO_2^-$
- ► *hexadentate* ligand consists of many atoms, six of which are each capable of forming one dative bond with the central ion: e.g. EDTA (EthyleneDiamineTetraAcetate).

Shape of complex ions
Octahedral, square planar, tetrahedral and linear. Octahedral is most common and can give rise to geometrical and optical isomeric complexes.

REVISION ACTIVITY

Multiple choice questions

1 Which one of the following is a nucleophile?

    A $AlCl_3$ **B** BF_3 **C** H_2O **D** NO_2^+

2 Which one of the following is the correct order of **increasing** solubility?

    A $Mg(OH)_2$ $Ca(OH)_2$ $Ba(OH)_2$ **C** $Ba(OH)_2$ $Mg(OH)_2$ $Ca(OH)_2$
    B $MgSO_4$ $CaSO_4$ $BaSO_4$ **D** $BaSO_4$ $MgSO_4$ $CaSO_4$

3 Which one of the following is the atomic number of a 3d transition element with a single 4s electron in its ground state atom?

    A 22   **B** 23   **C** 24   **D** 25

4 Aqueous silver nitrate reacts with one mole of a cobalt(II) complex to give 2 mol AgCl. Which one of the following is the most likely formula for the complex?

    A $[Co(NH_3)_6]Cl_2$ **C** $[Co(NH_3)_4(H_2O)_2]Cl_3$
    B $[Co(NH_3)_5Cl]Cl_2$ **D** $[Co(NH_3)_4(H_2O)Cl]Cl_2$

5 Which one of the following when added to water does **NOT** produce fumes of hydrogen chloride?

    A Aluminium chloride Al_2Cl_6 **C** Lithium chloride LiCl
    B Boron trichloride BCl_3 **D** Silicon tetrachloride $SiCl_4$

Grid question

A	B	C
ammonia NH_3	water H_2O	hydrogen fluoride HF
D	**E**	**F**
phosphine PH_3	hydrogen sulphide H_2S	hydrogen chloride HCl

(a) Identify the hydride with the highest boiling point.
(b) Identify the hydride which forms a strong acid when dissolved in water.
(c) Identify the hydride(s) which form a weak acid when dissolved in water.
(d) Identify the hydride(s) which produce a precipitate with aqueous copper(II) ions.

Multiple completion question

answer choice
A = (i)(ii)(iii)
B = (i)(iii)
C = (ii)(iv)
D = (iv)

Which of the following would react with water to form a basic hydroxide?

    (i) Lithium hydride LiH
    (ii) Magnesium hydride MgH_2
    (iii) Sodium oxide Na_2O
    (iv) Silicon dioxide SiO_2

EXAMINATION QUESTIONS

Question 1

This question concerns patterns in the properties of the hydrides, oxides and chlorides of elements shown in the following portion of the Periodic Table.

Li	Be	B	C
Na	Mg	Al	Si	P	S	Cl	Ar
			Ge
			Sn
			Pb

HINT
Can you count up to four?

(a) Using only those elements listed above
    (i) give the formula of an ionic hydride: .... [1]
    (ii) give the formula of a diatomic covalent hydride and explain why it is polar

    .... [2]

    (iii) give the formula of a non-polar covalent hydride and explain why it is non-polar

    .... [2]

    (iv) give the equation for the reaction of a diatomic hydride with water to form an alkaline solution:

    .... [2]

(b) State how the acid–base character of the oxides changes across the period from sodium to chlorine and illustrate your statement by writing an equation for an appropriate reaction for each of the following oxides.

    statement..

    .... [1]

    sodium oxide .... [1]

    sulphur dioxide .... [1]

(c) Describe a *trend* in the properties, *down the group* from carbon to lead, of
    (i) the oxides CO_2, SiO_2, SnO_2, PbO_2

    ....

    .... [2]

    (ii) the chlorides CCl_4, $SiCl_4$, $SnCl_4$, $PbCl_4$

    ....

    .... [2]

(d) Compare the reactions of sodium chloride, aluminium chloride and silicon chloride with water to illustrate how the ease of hydrolysis varies across the period Na to Ar.

    ....

    ....

    .... [3]

(e) *There is a diagonal relationship between lithium and magnesium.* Explain what is meant by this statement and illustrate your answer by reference to the chlorides.

    ....

    ....

    .... [3]

    total 20 marks

Question 2

This question concerns the s-block elements and their compounds.

(a) State the trend in the solubilities of the sulphates of Group 2 with increasing atomic number and give a reason for the trend.

Trend.. [1]

Reason for trend..

.... [1]

HINT
Say what you see, not what you think is happening

(b) Describe what you would **observe** if samples of potassium nitrate and magnesium nitrate were heated separately in a test tube.

potassium nitrate...

....

.... [2]

magnesium nitrate..

....

.... [2]

(c) Suggest a reason why

(i) lithium forms a hydrated chloride ($LiCl.H_2O$) but the other alkali metals in Group 1 of the Periodic Table form only an anhydrous chloride.

....

....

....

.... [2]

(ii) anhydrous magnesium carbonate decomposes when heated to 350 °C but anhydrous sodium carbonate only melts when heated to 850 °C.

....

....

....

.... [2]

(d) Explain, with the help of suitable equations, why

(i) aqueous sodium carbonate is strongly alkaline;

....

....

....

.... [2]

(ii) the aqueous hydrogencarbonate ion concentration increases when rain water passes through limestone.

....

....

....

.... [2]

total 14 marks

Question 3

(a) Aluminium powder can be used to reduce iron(III) oxide in the 'thermit' reaction.

(i) Write a balanced equation for the reaction.

.... [1]

(ii) Calculate the enthalpy change for the above reaction given that the standard enthalpy change of formation of aluminium oxide is $-1669\,kJ\,mol^{-1}$ and that of iron(III) oxide is $-822\,kJ\,mol^{-1}$.

....

.... [1]

(iii) Explain why metallic aluminium reacts very little with moist air even though the standard reduction potential for aluminium is $-1.66\,V$.

....

.... [1]

(b) (i) Explain why aqueous aluminium sulphate is acidic.

....

....

.... [2]

(ii) Describe what happens when aqueous sodium carbonate is added to aqueous aluminium sulphate.

....

....

.... [2]

(iii) Explain, with the help of ionic equations, what happens to aqueous aluminium sulphate when drops of aqueous sodium hydroxide are added until in excess.

....

....

....

.... [4]

(c) (i) Write the formula of the anion in sodium hexafluoroaluminate(III).

.... [1]

(ii) State one industrial use for sodium hexafluoroaluminate(III).

.... [1]

(d) (i) Write the formula of the anion in sodium tetrahydridoborate(III).

.... [1]

(ii) State one laboratory use for sodium tetrahydridoborate(III).

.... [1]

total 15 marks

HINT
Count the marks and watch your time

Question 4

(a) Some of the oxides of the Group 4 elements are shown in the table below.

CO_2 CO	SiO_2	GeO_2	SnO_2	PbO PbO_2

From these oxides choose

(i) an oxide with a giant covalent structure .... [1]

(ii) the oxide which has the most basic character .... [1]

(iii) an oxide which will oxidize concentrated hydrochloric acid .... [1]

(iv) a strongly reducing oxide .... [1]

(b) Some of the chlorides of the Group 4 elements are shown in the table below.

CCl_4	$SiCl_4$	$GeCl_4$	$SnCl_2$ $SnCl_4$	$PbCl_2$ $PbCl_4$

(i) State and explain the difference in the behaviour of tetrachloromethane and silicon tetrachloride towards water.

....

....

....

.... [3]

(ii) Explain the existence of the dichlorides tin and lead in terms of *the inert pair effect*.

....

....

.... [3]

(iii) Write an equation to represent the reaction of $PbCl_4$ with water.

.... [1]

HINT

Can ⇌ ever be replaced by →?

(c) When tin(II) chloride is dissolved in water the solution becomes cloudy with a white precipitate

$$SnCl_2(s) + H_2O(l) \rightarrow Sn(OH)Cl(s) + HCl(aq)$$

(i) Explain why aqueous tin(II) chloride is usually made up in hydrochloric acid.

....

....

.... [2]

(ii) Aqueous tin(II) chloride is a strong reducing agent. Write an equation for the reaction of aqueous tin(II) chloride with aqueous iron(III) chloride.

.... [1]

(iii) Explain why aqueous solutions of tin(II) chloride are stored in contact with metallic tin.

.... [1]

total 15 marks

Question 5

HINT

Why only one mark for the first sodium halide?

(a) Describe what is observed when small samples of solid sodium chloride, solid sodium bromide and solid sodium iodide are warmed separately with concentrated sulphuric acid.

sodium chloride...

....

.... [1]

sodium bromide...

....

.... [2]

sodium iodide...

....

.... [2]

(b) The reaction of chlorine with aqueous sodium hydroxide under different conditions is represented by the following ionic equations.

I With cold dilute sodium hydroxide:

$$Cl_2(g) + 2OH^-(aq) \rightarrow Cl^-(aq) + ClO^-(aq) + H_2O(l)$$

II With hot concentrated sodium hydroxide:

$$3Cl_2(g) + 6OH^-(aq) \rightarrow 5Cl^-(aq) + ClO_3^-(aq) + 3H_2O(l)$$

(i) What type of reaction is represented by the above ionic equations?

.... [1]

(ii) Give the name of the oxo anions of chlorine formed in the reactions.

ClO^- .... ClO_3^- .... [2]

(iii) Give **one** everyday use for **each** of the following reaction products.

NaClO .... [1]

$NaClO_3$ .... [1]

(c) Fluorine is the first member of Group 7. Some of its properties are different from those of the other halogens. Illustrate **two** of these differences by reference to

(i) the acidity of the aqueous hydrogen halides

....

.... [1]

(ii) the solubilities of the silver halides

....

.... [1]

total 12 marks

Question 6

(a) The first-row elements in the d-block of the Periodic Table are shown below. Except for scandium (atomic number 21) and zinc, the elements are typical transition metals.

Sc	Ti	V	Cr	Mn	Fe	Co	Ni	Cu	Zn

(i) Write the ground state electronic configuration, in terms of s, p and d electrons, for zinc and give one reason why the element is not a typical transition metal.

Electronic configuration ....

Reason .... [2]

(ii) One characteristic property of a transition metal is the ability to exist in two or more oxidation states. To illustrate this property, choose **one** of the above transition metals and give the formula of an ion or compound for the following oxidation states:

Oxidation state	+2	+3	+4	+5
Formula of ion or compound	....	....	....	....

[4]

(iii) State **four** other general characteristic properties of transition metals.

....

....

....

.... [4]

(b) Compounds such as potassium dichromate(VI) in which the transition element has a high oxidation state tend to be strong oxidizing agents.

(i) Write an ion/electron half equation for the reduction of dichromate(VI) ions in acidic aqueous solution.

.... [1]

(ii) Write a balanced ionic equation for the oxidation of iron(II) ions by dichromate(VI) ions in acidic aqueous solution.

.... [1]

(c) $30 \, cm^3$ of aqueous potassium dichromate(VI) of concentration $0.02 \, mol \, dm^{-3}$ are required to oxidize $25 \, cm^3$ of acidic aqueous iron(II) sulphate. Calculate the concentration of the iron(II) sulphate solution.

....

....

....

.... [2]

total 14 marks

HINT

Read all the parts of the question before you start writing

7 Organic chemistry

Organic chemistry
Study of carbon compounds.

Formulae
There are five types of organic formulae: **empirical** simplest C_2H_4O

molecular $n \times$ empirical   **displayed** or **graphic**   **stereochemical** or **spatial**

$$C_4H_8O_2$$

'3-D perspective' diagram

structural
$(CH_3)_2CHCO_2H$

Isomerism
Existence of two or more compounds with the same molecular formula but different physical and/or chemical properties.

Study Guide
Chapter 14

Types of Isomerism

▶ **chain isomers**

$CH_3-CH_2-CH_2-CH_2-CH_3$ $CH_3-\overset{\overset{\displaystyle CH_3}{|}}{C}H-CH_2-CH_3$ $CH_3-\overset{\overset{\displaystyle CH_3}{|}}{\underset{\underset{\displaystyle CH_3}{|}}{C}}H-CH_2-CH_3$

         pentane   2-methylbutane   2,2-dimethylpropane

▶ **position isomers**

$CH_3-CH_2-CH_2-CH_2-\overset{\overset{\displaystyle Br}{|}}{C}H_2$ $CH_3-CH_2-CH_2-\overset{\overset{\displaystyle Br}{|}}{C}H-CH_3$ $CH_3-CH_2-\overset{\overset{\displaystyle Br}{|}}{C}H-CH_2-CH_3$

     1-bromopentane   2-bromopentane   3-bromopentane

▶ **metamers**

$CH_3-CH_2-CH_2-CO_2-CH_3$ $CH_3-CH_2-CO_2-CH_2-CH_3$ $CH_3-CO_2-CH_2-CH_2-CH_3$

     methylbutanoate   ethylpropanoate   propylethanoate

▶ **functional group isomers**

     $CH_3-CH_2-CH_2-CH_2-OH$ butan-1-ol CH_3-CH_2-CHO propanal

     $CH_3-CH_2-O-CH_2-CH_3$ ethoxyethane $CH_3-CO-CH_3$ propanone

▶ **nuclear isomers**   ▶ **geometric isomers**

2-methylphenol   3-methylphenol   4-methylphenol

(*ortho*-cresol)   (*meta*-cresol)   (*para*-cresol)

                                         cis-   *trans-*

                                          1,2-dichloroethene

▶ **enantiomers (optical isomers)**

chiral centre: asymmetric carbon atom with four different atoms or groups attached

L-(+)-alanine   L-(−)-alanine
2-aminopropanoic acid

Nomenclature

Systematic naming (consisting of prefix(es), root and suffix together with numbers and punctuation) based on the structure of the organic compounds.

Homologous series

▶ general formula (e.g. carboxylic acids $C_nH_{2n+1}CO_2H$)
▶ successive homologues differ by CH_2 **but**
▶ each has same functional group ($-CO_2H$)
▶ therefore similar chemical properties **but**
▶ trend in physical properties with increasing chain length
Trends in properties of a series may be explained in terms of the change in inter-molecular forces and molecular complexity with increasing molecular size: e.g. alkan-1-ols ($C_nH_{2n+1}OH$) show with increasing value of n
  – increase in b.pt. (increasing van der Waals forces)
  – decrease in reactivity with sodium (OH group masked by HC chain).

Functional group

An element (e.g. Br) or group of elements (e.g. OH) responsible for specific properties of an organic compound or class of compounds.

functional group		suffix	class	reacts with
>C:C<	>C=C<	ene	alkenes	electrophiles (e.g. Br_2)
C_6H_5	⬡	benzene	arenes	electrophiles (e.g. NO_2^+)
−OH	−O—H	ol	alcohols; phenols	Na; PCl_5; MnO_4^-/H^+
−NH₂	−N(H)(H)	amine	primary amines	electrophiles
−CHO	−C(=O)(H)	al	aldehydes	nucleophiles
>CO	−C(=O)\	one	ketones & aldehydes	nucleophiles
−CO₂H	−C(=O)(O—H)	oic acid	carboxylic acids	alcohols, bases, metals, phosphorus halides
−COCl	−C(=O)(Cl)	oyl chloride	acyl chlorides	−OH, −NH₂ groups
−CN	−C≡N	nitrile	nitriles	aqueous acid or alkali
−Hal	−F, −Cl, −Br, −I		halogeno compounds	aqueous or alcoholic OH⁻ and CN⁻; −NH₂ group

Study Guide Chapter 15 to 20 for the reactions of the functional groups

Types of bond breaking

$$-\overset{|}{\underset{|}{C}} - \overset{|}{\underset{|}{C}} - \longrightarrow -\overset{|}{\underset{|}{C}}\cdot \quad \cdot\overset{|}{\underset{|}{C}}-$$

homolytic fission into free radicals

$$-\overset{|}{\underset{|}{C}} - Cl \longrightarrow -\overset{|}{\underset{|}{C}}^+ \quad Cl^-$$

heterolytic fission into ions

Types of reaction

▶ *Addition*   an atom or group is added to a molecule
▶ *Elimination*   an atom or group is removed from a molecule
▶ *Rearrangement*   atoms or groups in a molecule change position

▶ *Substitution*   one atom or group in a molecule replaced by another atom or group
▶ *Condensation*   addition followed by elimination

Types of reacting species
▶ *Electrophile*   an electron-pair acceptor (Lewis acid).
▶ *Nucleophile*   an electron-pair donor (Lewis base).

Reaction mechanisms
▶ *nucleophilic attack upon electrophilic centres*
  – nucleophilic substitution
    (alkaline hydrolysis of halogenoalkanes)

  – electrophilic substitution
    (halogen carrier bromination of benzene)

  – electrophilic addition to alkenes in the absence of UV light (Markovnikov's rule)

  – nucleophilic addition of ammonia to electrophilic carbon atom in the carbonyl group

▶ *free radical chain reactions*

	bromination of methane	polymerization of ethene
initiation	$Br_2 \rightarrow 2Br\cdot$	$X{-}X \rightarrow 2X\cdot$
propagation	$Br\cdot + CH_4 \rightarrow HBr + \cdot CH_3$	$X\cdot + C_2H_4 \rightarrow XCH_2CH_2\cdot$
	$Br_2 + \cdot CH_3 \rightarrow CH_3Br + Br\cdot$	$X(CH_2)_2\cdot + C_2H_4 \rightarrow X(CH_2)_4\cdot$
termination	$\cdot CH_3 + \cdot CH_3 \rightarrow C_2H_6$	$X\cdot + X(CH_2)_n\cdot \rightarrow X(CH_2)_nX$

Polymerization
Combining of a large number of small molecules (monomers) to form a small number of large molecules (polymers).

▶ *Addition polymerization* Combining of unsaturated monomers (usually alkenes) to form saturated polymers (usually alkanes).
▶ *Condensation polymerization* Combining of monomers (e.g. di-ols and dicarboxylic acids) with the elimination of a small molecule (e.g. H_2O).

Condensation polymers
▶ *polyesters*

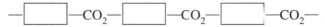

▶ *polyamides* (nylons)

⭐ **REVISION ACTIVITY**

Multiple choice questions

1 Which one of the following would produce a colour change with aqueous iron(III) chloride?

 A ethanol **B** phenol **C** phenylmethanol **D** phenyl ethanoate

2 In the electrophilic substitution of benzene by chlorine in the presence of a halogen carrier, the halogen carrier is

 A an electrophile **B** a nucleophile **C** a free radical **D** a negative ion

3 The reaction of bromine with propene is best described as

 A electrophilic addition   **C** nucleophilic addition
 B electrophilic substitution   **D** nucleophilic substitution

4 Which one of the following is **least likely** to be formed by bubbling gaseous ethene into a mixture of aqueous bromine and aqueous sodium chloride?

 A CH_2BrCH_2Br **C** CH_2BrCH_2OH
 B CH_2BrCH_2Cl **D** CH_2ClCH_2Cl

5 Which one of the following is **not** an addition polymer?

 A Nylon   **B** Polystyrene   **C** Polythene   **D** PVC

Grid question

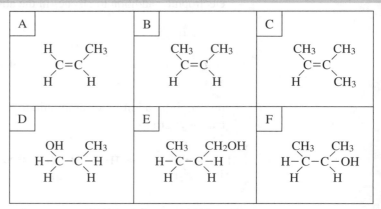

Identify the structure(s) of a molecule:
(a) that has a chiral centre   (c) that oxidizes to an aldehyde
(b) that oxidizes to a ketone   (d) that can exhibit geometric isomerism

Multiple completion question

answer choice
A = (i)(ii)(iii)
B = (i)(iii)
C = (ii)(iv)
D = (iv)

Which of the following terms would apply to the hydrolysis of 1-bromobutane by aqueous sodium hydroxide?

 (i) addition/elimination
 (ii) electrophilic substitution
 (iii) nucleophilic addition
 (iv) nucleophilic substitution

EXAMINATION QUESTIONS

Question 1

(a) (i) Draw the structures for the geometric isomers *cis*-but-2-ene and *trans*-but-2-ene.

         cis-but-2-ene   *trans*-but-2-ene   [2]

  (ii) State and explain by reference only to the above **structures**, which of the two isomers would be expected to be the more stable energetically.

....

.... [2]

(b) *Cis*-but-2-ene slowly isomerizes to *trans*-but-2-ene. The reaction is catalysed by iodine. The first two steps in the mechanism may be as follows.

$$I_2 \longrightarrow 2I\cdot$$

$$I\cdot \;+\; \underset{H}{\overset{CH_3}{C}}=\underset{H}{\overset{CH_3}{C}} \longrightarrow I-\underset{H}{\overset{CH_3}{C}}-\underset{H}{\overset{CH_3}{C\cdot}}$$

      step 1   step 2

  (i) What name is given to the type of bond breaking represented in step 1?

.... [1]

  (ii) Give the name of the species represented by I· and by the product in step 2.

.... [1]

  (iii) Write an equation to show the formation of *trans*-but-2-ene from the intermediate produced in step 2.

                                                       [2]

  (iv) What property of the structure of the intermediate enables *cis*-but-2-ene to change into *trans*-but-2-ene?

.... [1]

(c) *cis*-butenedioic acid and *trans*-butenedioic acid are geometric isomers. Only one of them readily forms the anhydride of butenedioic. Both react with gaseous hydrogen in the presence of Raney nickel but only one product is formed. Both react with with hydrogen bromide yielding two isomers.

  (i) Predict which of the geometric isomers would form the anhydride and explain your reasoning.

....

.... [2]

  (ii) Explain the reactions with hydrogen and with hydrogen bromide.

....

....

....

....

....

.... [4]

total 15 marks

HINT

What's the point of a dot?

Question 2

(a) What is meant by the terms *nucleophile* and *electrophile*?

Nucleophile ....

.... [1]

Electrophile ....

.... [1]

(b) The hydrolysis of 1-bromobutane by aqueous sodium hydroxide to form butan-1-ol is said to be an example of nucleophilic substitution.
(i) Show the mechanism of this reaction.

[3]

(ii) What experimental evidence is available to support this mechanism?

....

.... [2]

HINT
Reactions in test tubes should be simple.

(c) 1-bromobutane and bromobenzene are colourless liquids. Describe a test-tube reaction by which you could distinguish between separate samples of the liquids.

....

....

.... [4]

(d) The action of ultraviolet light on *CFCs* in the Earth's stratosphere may release chlorine *radicals* and cause holes in the ozone layer by a two-step reaction as follows:

step 1: $Cl\cdot + O_3 \rightarrow ClO\cdot + O_2$

step 2: $ClO\cdot + O_3 \rightarrow Cl\cdot + 2O_2$

(i) What is meant by the terms *radical* and *CFC*?

Radical...

.... [1]

CFC...

.... [1]

(ii) Write an equation for the formation of a chlorine radical from a CFC.

.... [1]

(iii) Write the equation for the overall reaction represented by steps 1 and 2 above.

.... [1]

(iv) State and explain the function of the chlorine radical in the overall reaction.

....

.... [2]

total 17 marks

Question 3

This question concerns organic compounds containing oxygen.

(a) Draw structures for the following functional groups.

    (i) Aldehyde   (ii) Ketone

    (iii) Carboxyl   (iv) Secondary alcohol

[4]

> **HINT**
>
> *Do functional groups always function?*

(b) Describe test-tube reactions to distinguish between the two compounds in each of the following pairs. Your answers should state the effect on **each** compound.

    (i) Ethanol and propanone

....

.... [2]

    (ii) Propanal and propanone

....

.... [2]

    (iii) Propan-1-ol and propan-2-ol

....

.... [2]

    (iv) Benzoic acid and phenol

....

.... [2]

(c) Ethyl ethanoate may be formed by reacting ethanol **either** with ethanoic acid under suitable conditions **or** with ethanoyl chloride.

    (i) State the conditions for the reaction between ethanol and ethanoic acid.

....

.... [2]

    (ii) Write a balanced equation for this reaction.

.... [1]

    (iii) Write a balanced equation for the reaction of ethanoyl chloride with ethanol.

.... [1]

    (iv) Draw the structural formula of ethyl ethanoate.

[1]

total 17 marks

Question 4

(a) By drawing structures, distinguish between primary, secondary and tertiary amines.

[3]

(b) The germicide, cetyltrimethylammonium bromide (cetrimide), has the formula $CH_3(CH_2)_{15}N(CH_3)_3Br$. It is an ionic quaternary ammonium compound which can be prepared by reacting trimethylamine with 1-bromohexadecane (cetyl bromide).

(i) What would you expect to see if an aqueous solution of cetrimide were treated with aqueous silver nitrate?

.... [1]

(ii) Write down the structure of cetyl bromide.

HINT
Why are there NO lines?

[1]

(iii) Write a balanced equation for the reaction of trimethylamine with cetyl bromide.

.... [1]

(c) Primary amines yield nitrogen quantitatively when treated with nitrous acid.

(i) Write an equation for the reaction of nitrous acid with 3-aminopentane.

[1]

(ii) What volume of nitrogen measured at s.t.p. would be obtained quantitatively by treating 8.7 g of 3-aminopentane with excess nitrous acid?

$A_r(H) = 1$; $A_r(C) = 12$; $A_r(N) = 14$. Molar volume at s.t.p. $= 22.4\,dm^3\,mol^{-1}$.

....

....

.... [2]

(d) Lithium tetrahydridoaluminate(III) will reduce nitriles to primary amines and isonitriles to secondary amines. Give the name and structural formula of the **amine** formed by reduction of the compounds with the following formulae.

compound to be reduced C_6H_5CN C_2H_5NC

name of amine formed   ....

structure of amine

[4]

total 13 marks

Question 5

(a) An important industrial process uses the following three-stage reaction sequence.

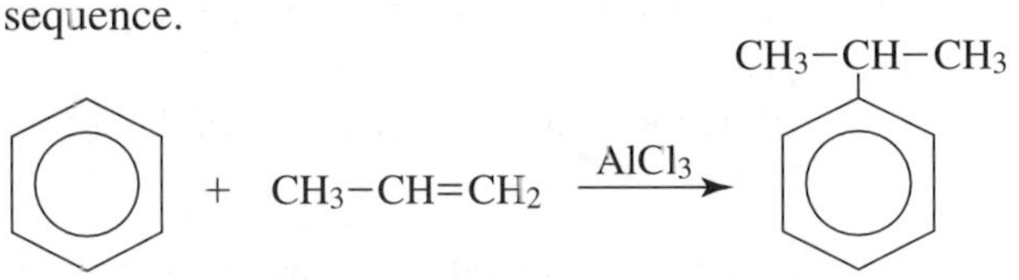

(i) Give the name and state the type of reaction in the first stage of the process.

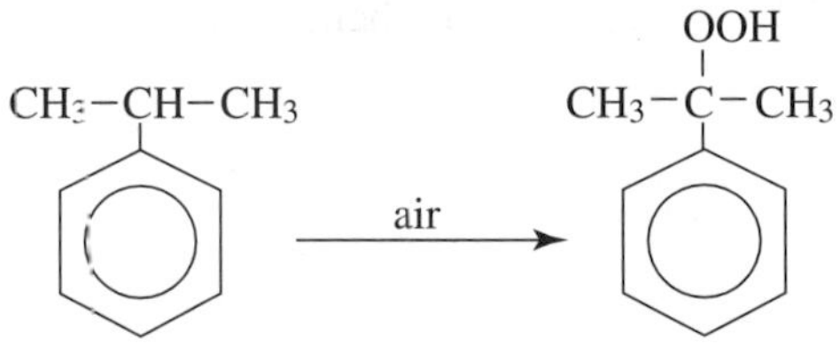

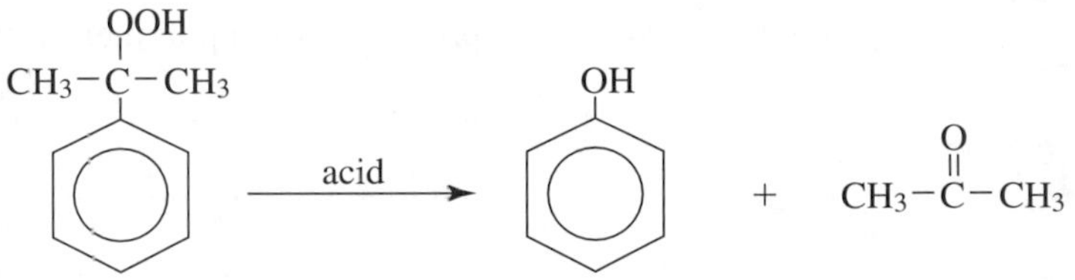

name...

type of reaction.. [2]

(ii) Give the name of the chemicals labelled **I** to **IV**.

I .... **III** ....

II .... **IV** .... [4]

(iii) What is the major source of the starting materials?

.... [1]

(b) Give the structures of the products formed when compound **III** reacts with

(i) aqueous sodium hydroxide

HINT
How much time do you have for this whole question?

(ii) aqueous bromine.

[2]

total 9 marks

Question 6

(a) Poly(tetrafluoroethene) is an addition polymer produced by free radical polymerization of tetrafluoroethene using an initiator of ammonium peroxosulphate.

(i) What is the purpose of the initiator?

.... [1]

(ii) Draw structural formulae to show the bonds in a molecule of tetrafluoroethene and in part of a poly(tetrafluoroethene) chain with at least four carbon atoms.

tetrafluoroethene molecule   poly(tetrafluoroethene) polymer chain

[2]

(iii) Give an everyday use for poly(tetrafluoroethene) and state the physical property of the polymer on which this use depends.

....

....

.... [2]

(b) The names *'Terylene'* and *'Dacron'* refer to polyesters derived from benzene-1,4-dicarboxylic acid and ethane-1,2-diol. *Nylon-6* refers to a polyamide derived from caprolactam whose structure is shown on the right. Polyesters and polyamides are condensation polymers.

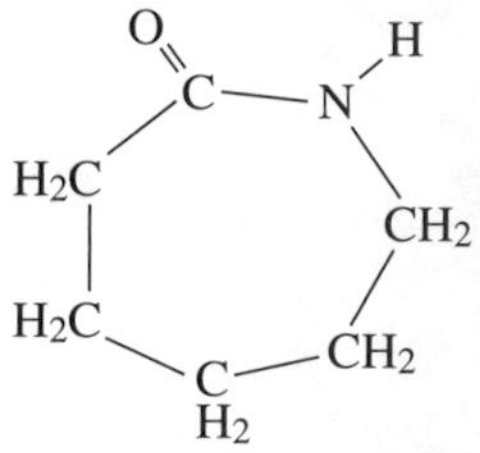

(i) Draw structural formulae to show the bonds in a molecule of ethane-1, 2-diol and in a molecule of benzene-1,4-dicarboxylic acid.
   ethane-1,2-diol: *benzene-1,4-dicarboxylic acid:*

[3]

(ii) Draw a structural formula to show all the bonds in the ester linkage of polyesters.

[1]

(iii) Draw a structural formula, derived from two caprolactam molecules, to show part of the chain of *Nylon-6*.

[2]

(iv) Give two large-scale uses for condensation polymers.

....

.... [2]

total 13 marks

TOP HINT
ALWAYS READ THE QUESTION AND GIVE ONLY THE ANSWER REQUIRED.

part III
Answers and tips for topics 1 to 7

Solutions
Revision activities topics 1 to 7

SOLUTIONS TO REVISION ACTIVITIES

Multiple choice answers

Topic 1	Topic 2	Topic 3	Topic 4	Topic 5	Topic 6	Topic 7
1 C	1 D	1 C	1 C	1 A	1 C	1 B
2 C	2 A	2 B	2 D	2 C	2 A	2 A
3 D	3 C	3 C	3 D	3 A	3 C	3 A
4 A	4 B	4 D	4 A	4 D	4 A	4 D
5 C	5 B		5 B	5 B	5 C	5 A

Grid answers

Topic 1	Topic 2	Topic 3	Topic 4	Topic 5	Topic 6	Topic 7
(a) E	(a) BF	(a) CF	(a) AE	(a) ACE	(a) B	(a) F
(b) B	(b) AD	(b) BDF	(b) CF	(b) DBF	(b) F	(b) F
(c) C		(c) AE	(c) BD		(c) CE	(c) DE
(d) F					(d) ADE	(d) B

Multiple completion answers

Topic 1	Topic 2	Topic 3	Topic 4	Topic 5	Topic 6	Topic 7
C	D	D	B	C	A	D

Solutions
Examination answers

TOPIC 1 Structure and bonding

Question 1

Tip Make sure your definition of A_r refers to isotopic composition and to ^{12}C.

(a) *Mass number* (A) is the number of protons (Z) and neutrons in the nucleus of a nuclide. *Relative atomic mass* (A_r) is the ratio of the average mass per atom of the natural isotopic composition of an element to one-twelfth of the mass of an atom of nuclide ^{12}C. The superscript ^{12} is the mass number of the nuclide.
(3 marks)

Tip A probability is always a fraction and the sum of the probabilities must equal 1.

(b) Chlorine contains two isotopes ^{35}Cl and ^{37}Cl in the ratio of 3:1.
    (i) 0.75 or 3 in 4 *(1 mark)*
    (ii) $0.75 \times 0.75 = 0.5625$ or 9 in 16 *(1 mark)*
    (iii) $0.25 \times 0.25 = 0.0625$ or 1 in 16 *(1 mark)*
    (iv) $1 - (0.5625 + 0.0625) = 0.375$ or 6 in 16 *(1 mark)*

    (v)

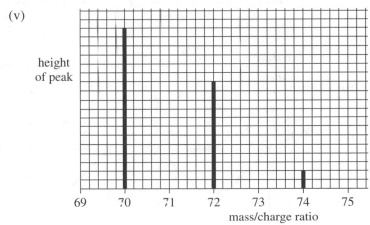

(2 marks)

(c) (i) $^{14}_{6}C \rightarrow {}^{14}_{7}N + \beta$ *(2 marks)*
    (ii) 1 half-life (5600 years) $\rightarrow$ 50%; 2 half-lives $\rightarrow$ 25%; 3 half-lives $\rightarrow$ 12.5%.
    So, approximate age of artefact is $3 \times 5600 = 16\,800$ years old. *(2 marks)*
(total 13 marks)

Question 2

Tip Watch out for Cr and Cu because the stability of a d-shell half-filled or filled means 1 electron in the 4s orbital.

(a) (i) Cl $1s^2 2s^2 2p^6 3s^2 3p^5$ *(1 mark)*
    (ii) Ca $1s^2 2s^2 2p^6 3s^2 3p^6 4s^2$ *(1 mark)*
    (iii) Cr $1s^2 2s^2 2p^6 3s^2 3p^6 3d^5 4s^1$ *(1 mark)*

(b) (i) *(1 mark)* (ii) *(1 mark)* (iii) *(2 marks)*

  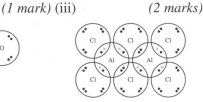

(c) (i) In sodium chloride, each ion is   In caesium chloride, each ion is
         surrounded by **six** of the oppositely   surrounded by **eight** of the oppositely
         charged ions. Sodium chloride has a   charged ions. Caesium chloride has a
         double interlocking **face-centred**   double interlocking **simple** cubic
         cubic structure.   structure.

Tip Avoid taking up time
drawing complicated diagrams
when a simple one will do!

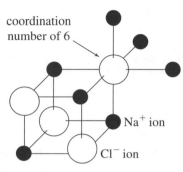

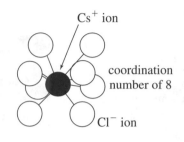

                                    (2 marks)   *(2 marks)*
(ii) The caesium cation is much larger than the sodium cation.   *(1 mark)*
                                                                   (total 12 marks)

Question 3

(a)

Molecule	Number of bonding electron pairs	Number of non-bonding electron pairs	Shape of molecule
BF_3	3	0	trigonal planar
NH_3	3	1	pyramidal
SF_6	6	0	octahedral
H_2O	2	2	bent

(4 marks)

Tip For pyramidal, octahedral,
tetrahedral and trigonal
bipyramidal structures your
drawing must look
three-dimensional to
gain full marks.

(b)

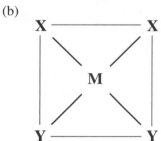 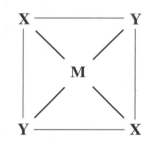 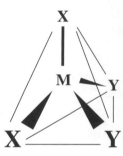

   cis isomer   *trans* isomer   tetrahedral
   X-atoms different distances apart
   in the two square planar structures
               (2 marks)   *(1 mark)*

(c) (i) **diamond**   **iodine**
         extremely hard   very soft
         extremely high melting point   low melting point   *(2 marks)*
    (ii) all the carbon atoms are   pairs of atoms are strongly held together
         strongly held together by   by single covalent bonds into diatomic
         four covalent bonds per   molecules but these small molecules are
         atom into one giant three-   attracted to each other only by weak van
         dimensional structure.   der Waals forces.
                       (1 mark)   *(2 marks)*
                                                                  (total 12 marks)

TOPIC 2 Energetics

Question 1

(a) Use a more accurate (narrower temperature range) thermometer
Clamp the calorimeter directly over the burner and discard the gauze and tripod
Shield the apparatus from air draughts
Stir the water (carefully, using the thermometer)   *(4 marks)*

Tip If you show your working you may get some marks even if your final answer is wrong.

(b) (i) heat capacity of apparatus is $120 \times 0.387 + 100 \times 4.18 = 464.4\,\mathrm{J\,K^{-1}}$

rise in temperature is $75 - 20 = 55\,\mathrm{K}$

heat evolved is $464.4 \times 55 = 25\,542\,\mathrm{J}$

mass of ethanol burnt is $43.56 - 41.36 = 2.20\,\mathrm{g}$

amount of ethanol burnt is $2.20/46.1 = 0.0477\,\mathrm{mol}$

Tip Using the calculator without intermediate steps gives the number 535267.1 but even 535 may give too many significant figures in the answer and lose a mark.

molar enthalpy change is $25\,542/0.0477 = -535\,000\,\mathrm{J} = -535\,\mathrm{kJ}$ *(4 marks)*

(ii) The student's value shows not enough heat has been transferred to the calorimeter and its contents, possibly because heat was lost to the gauze, tripod and surrounding air *(1)*, combustion was incomplete *(1)*, some ethanol was lost by evaporation *(1)*, the reactants and products were not measured under standard temperature and pressure conditions *(1)*.   *(4 marks)*

(c) Complete combustion occurs when the sample is burnt in pure oxygen under high pressure but the reaction takes place at constant volume, so the heat change measured is an internal energy change, ΔU.   *(3 marks)*

(total 15 marks)

Question 2

temp/°C

$30 - 16$
$= 14\,°C$
rise in temp

Tip On graphs you often have to draw the best straight lines (use a ruler) to extrapolate for the values you need.

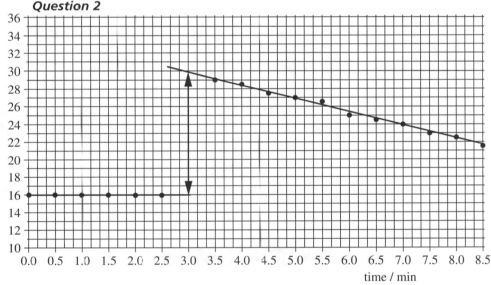

time / min

(a) Corrected temperature rise is $30 - 16 = 14\,°C$.   *(1 mark)*

(b) $2.0 \times (100\,\mathrm{cm^3}/1000\,\mathrm{cm^3}) = 0.20\,\mathrm{mol\,NaOH}$ *(1 mark)*

(c) Heat liberated is $4.2\,\mathrm{(J\,g^{-1}\,K^{-1})} \times 200\,\mathrm{(g)} \times 14\,\mathrm{(K)}$
        $= 11\,760\,\mathrm{J}$ by $0.20\,\mathrm{mol\,NaOH}$
So heat liberated per mole of NaOH is $11\,760/0.20 = 58\,800\,\mathrm{J}$
Hence molar enthalpy change of neutralization is $-58\,\mathrm{kJ\,mol^{-1}}$ *(2 marks)*

(d) $4.2 \times 300 \times \delta t / 0.2 = 58\,000$ where δt is temperature rise.
So δt is $(58\,000 \times 0.2) / (4.2 \times 300) = 9.2\,°C$
Hence highest temperature would be $16 + 9.2 = 25.2\,°C$ *(1 mark)*

(e) The hydrochloric acid and both alkalis are (strong electrolytes) completely dissociated in water, so the enthalpy change is for the neutralization reaction:
$H^+(aq) + OH^-(aq) \rightarrow H_2O(l)$ *(2 marks)*

(f) The reaction would be even more exothermic because the solid sodium hydroxide dissolves in water exothermically, heat being released as the hydroxide ions $OH^-(s)$ form hydrogen bonds with the water molecules to become hydrated $OH^-(aq)$ ions. *(2 marks)*

(total 9 marks)

Question 3

(a) (i) Using an energy cycle:

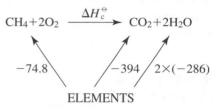

$$(-74.8) + \Delta H_c^{\ominus} = (-394) + 2 \times (-286)$$
So $\Delta H_c^{\ominus}$ is $(-394) + 2 \times (-286) - (-74.8) = -891.2\ kJ\ mol^{-1}$ *(2 marks)*

Tip Keep the $-$ and $+$ signs with the values in brackets until the final step. Lose the sign and you may lose the marks.

(ii) CH_4 $+\ 2O_2$ $\rightarrow$ CO_2 $+\ 2H_2O$
     $4 \times (+435)\ +\ 2 \times (+498)$ $2 \times (+805)\ +\ 2 \times\ [2 \times (+464)]$
So $\Delta H_c^{\ominus}$ is $-\{[2 \times (+805) + 2 \times 2 \times (+464)] - [4 \times (+435) + 2 \times (+498)]\}$
$$= -\{[1610 + 1856] - [1740 + 996]\}$$
$$= -730\ kJ\ mol^{-1}$$
                                     (2 marks)

Tip Don't forget that breaking bonds uses energy and therefore is endothermic with ΔH being positive.

(iii) The value $-891.2\ kJ\ mol^{-1}$ should be very close to the experimental value because the standard molar enthalpies of formation are obtained indirectly from experimentally determined enthalpies of combustion. The value $-730\ kJ\ mol^{-1}$ could be expected to differ from $-891.2\ kJ\ mol^{-1}$ because the bond dissociation energies are average energy values and may be determined by interpretation of data such as that obtained from spectroscopy.   *(2 marks)*

(b)

$$NaCl(s) \xrightarrow{\Delta H_{sol}} Na^+(aq) + Cl^-(aq)$$

$+787$ -406 -377

$$Na^+(g) \quad Cl^-(g)$$

$\Delta H_{sol} = (+787) + (-406) + (-377)$
So $\Delta H_{sol} = +4\ kJ\ mol^{-1}$ *(2 marks)*

(total 8 marks)

TOPIC 3   Kinetics

Question 1

(a) (i) (value at 5000 Pa) $140 - 0$ (value at 10 000 Pa) $= 140$ seconds
       (value at 3000 Pa) $250 - 110$ (value at 6000 Pa) $= 140$ seconds
       (value at 2000 Pa) $330 - 190$ (value at 4000 Pa) $= 140$ seconds   *(3 marks)*

(ii) The half-life is a constant (140 seconds) independent of the pressure (and therefore the concentration) of the dinitrogen pentoxide, so the reaction is first order with respect to the dinitrogen pentoxide.   *(2 marks)*

Tip Use $t_{\frac{1}{2}} \propto [\ ]^{(1-n)}$ to remember that for zero ($n=0$) order $t_{\frac{1}{2}}$ is directly proportional to $[\ ]$, for second order ($n=2$) it is inversely proportional to $[\ ]$ and for first ($n=1$) order $t_{\frac{1}{2}}$ is independent of $[\ ]$.

(b) (i) A tangent gives the change of pressure (dp) with time (dt) and is a measure of the decomposition rate ($-dp/dt$) at the point on the curve where the tangent is drawn.   *(1 mark)*

(ii) As the pressure decreases the slopes of the tangents become less negative: see sketch graph top of next page [The rate of decomposition is represented by the negative value of the slopes.]   *(2 marks)*

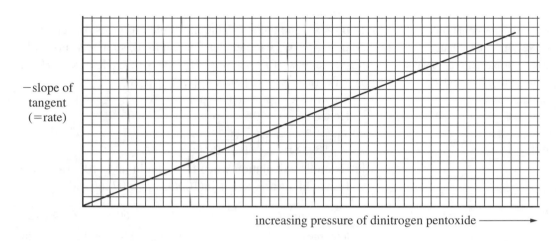

−slope of tangent (=rate)

increasing pressure of dinitrogen pentoxide ⟶

(total 8 marks)

Question 2

Tip Notice that the distribution curve gets lower and fatter as the temperature rises BUT the area under the curve does NOT change because it is proportional to the total number of molecules.

(a)

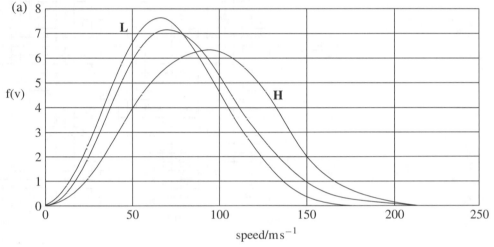

f(v)

speed/m s^{-1}

(2 marks)

(b)(i) The *activation energy* (E_a) is the minimum energy needed by reacting particles (atoms, ions or molecules) to achieve the transition state so that a reaction may occur between them. It is also a parameter in the Arrhenius equation for the dependence of the rate constant, k, upon temperature, T,
$k = Ae^{-(E_a/RT)}$ where A is a constant. *(1 mark)*

(ii)

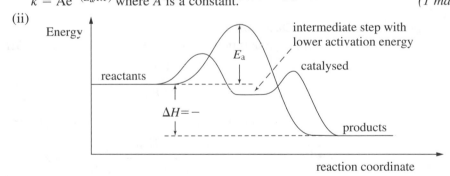

Energy

reactants

E_a

intermediate step with lower activation energy

catalysed

$\Delta H = -$

products

reaction coordinate

(2 marks)

(iii)   *(1 mark)*

(iv)A catalyst provides an alternate route for the reaction. This has the net effect of lowering the overall activation energy for the reaction. Consequently a greater proportion of the reacting particles (atoms, ions or molecules) will have this minimum energy, E_a, needed for a reaction to take place.

(4 marks)
(total 10 marks)

Question 3

Tip From the gas equation $pV = nRT$, it follows that p (pressure or partial pressure) is proportional to n if V and T are constant.

(a) (i) $p_e \propto x$ [one chloroethane molecule produces one ethene molecule] *(1 mark)*

(ii) $p_c \propto a - x$ [x molecules decomposed, so $a - x$ molecules left] *(1 mark)*

(iii) $p_t \propto a + x$ [$(a - x)$ of $C_2H_5Cl + x$ of $C_2H_4 + x$ of HCl molecules] *(1 mark)*

(b) (i) **x** is $\{(a + x) - a\}$ so $x \propto \{(p_t) - p_o\}$.

So, $a - x \propto p_o - (p_t - p_o)$

Hence $a - x \propto 2p_o - p_t$ *(2 marks)*

(ii) $\ln\left(\dfrac{a}{a-x}\right) = \ln\left(\dfrac{p_o}{2p_o - p_t}\right)$ *(1 mark)*

(iii) Example calculation when $t = 30$ min: $a = 100$, $(a - x)$ is $200 - 107 = 93$. Hence $\ln\{a/(a - x)\}$ is $\ln(100/93) = 0.0726$

time/min	0	30	60	90	120	150	180
total pressure/kPa	100	107	114	121	126	132	136
$\ln\{a/(a - x)\}$	0	0.0726	0.151	0.236	0.301	0.386	0.446

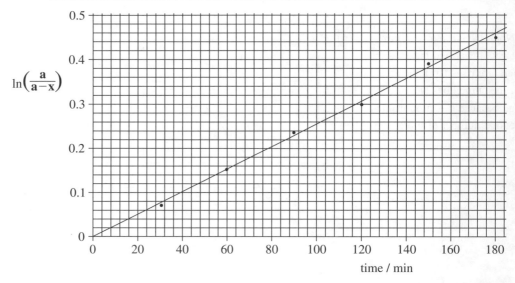

(4 marks)

(iv) $(0.46 - 0)/(180 - 0) = 2.6 \times 10^{-3}\,\text{min}^{-1}$. *(2 marks)*

(total 12 marks)

TOPIC 4 Chemical equilibria

Question 1

(a) (i) **reaction A**: $2SO_2(g) + O_2(g) \rightleftharpoons 2SO_3(g)$; $\Delta H^{\ominus} = -197\,\text{kJ mol}^{-1}$

$$\frac{[SO_3(g)]^2_{eqm}}{[SO_2(g)]^2_{eqm}[O_2(g)]_{eqm}} = K_c$$

reaction B: $H_2(g) + I_2(g) \rightleftharpoons 2HI(g)$; $\Delta H^{\ominus} = -9.6\,\text{kJ mol}^{-1}$

$$\frac{[HI(g)]^2_{eqm}}{[H_2(g)]_{eqm} \times [I_2(g)]_{eqm}} = K_c$$ *(2 marks)*

Tip Always remember that catalysts only change the rate to reach equilibrium. Catalysts NEVER alter the composition at equilibrium.

(ii) $K_p = K_c$ for reaction **B**. *(1 mark)*

(b) (i) increase total pressure = increase in equilibrium amount of sulphur trioxide

(ii) increase temperature = decrease in equilibrium amount of sulphur trioxide

(iii) add catalyst = no change in equilibrium amount of sulphur trioxide but reached more quickly

(iv) increase partial pressure of oxygen = increase in equilibrium amount of sulphur trioxide. *(4 marks)*

(c) (i) Haber-Bosch process   *(1 mark)*

(ii) Iron (finely divided and promoted by mixing with small amounts of oxides of potassium, calcium and aluminium) – a heterogeneous catalyst (in a different physical state from the reactants)   *(2 marks)*

(iii) Production of nitrogenous fertilizers (ammonium sulphate, ammonium nitrate). Production of nitric acid.   *(2 marks)*

                                                                                      (total 12 marks)

Question 2

(a) $pH = -\log_{10}([H^+(aq)]/\text{mol dm}^{-3})$ or the negative value of the logarithm, to the base ten, of the numerical value of the aqueous hydrogen ion concentration expressed in moles per cubic decimetre.   *(1 mark)*

(b) (i) $pH = 1.0$ *(1 mark)*

working: $-\log_{10}([H^+(aq)]/\text{mol dm}^{-3})$
$= -\log_{10}(0.1 \text{ mol dm}^{-3}/\text{mol dm}^{-3})$
$= -\log_{10}(0.1)$

(ii) $\dfrac{[H_3^+O(aq)][CH_3CO_2^-(aq)]}{[CH_3CO_2H(aq)]} = K_a = 1.8 \times 10^{-5} \text{ mol dm}^{-3}$

Tip By not ignoring the dissociation of the acid and by putting $[CH_3CO_2H(aq)] = 0.1 - [H^+(aq)]$, you have to solve a quadratic equation to get almost the same answer worth the same marks.

For this weak acid $[H^+(aq)]$ and $[CH_3CO_2^-(aq)]$ are approximately equal. The slight dissociation of the $CH_3CO_2H(aq)$ may be ignored so that $[CH_3CO_2H(aq)]$ is approximately $1.8 \times 10^{-5} \text{ mol dm}^{-3}$.

Therefore, $\dfrac{[H^+(aq)] \times [H^+(aq)]}{0.1} = 1.8 \times 10^{-5} \text{ mol dm}^{-3}$

$[H^+(aq)]^2 = 0.1 \times 1.8 \times 10^{-5} \text{ mol}^2 \text{ dm}^{-6}$

$[H^+(aq)] = \sqrt{1.8} \times 10^{-3} \text{ mol dm}^{-3}$ i.e. $1.34 \times 10^{-3} \text{ mol dm}^{-3}$

so $pH = 2.9$
working: $-\log_{10}(1.34 \times 10^{-3})$ is $-\{(-0.13) + (-3.00)\} = 2.87$ *(2 marks)*

(iii) $pK_a + pK_b = pK_w$.
So $9.25 + pK_b = 14$.
So $pK_b = 4.75 \rightarrow K_b = 1.8 \times 10^{-5} \text{ mol dm}^{-3}$

$\dfrac{[NH_4^+(aq)][OH^-(aq)]}{[NH_3 \cdot H_2O(aq)]} = K_b = 1.8 \times 10^{-5} \text{ mol dm}^{-3}$

Tip By not ignoring the dissociation of the base and by putting $[NH_3.H_2O(aq)] = 0.1 - [OH^-(aq)]$, you have to solve a quadratic equation to get almost the same answer worth the same marks.

For this weak base $[NH_4^+(aq)]$ and $[OH^-(aq)]$ are approximately equal. The slight dissociation of the $NH_3.H_2O(aq)$ may be ignored.
Therefore, $\dfrac{[OH^-(aq)] \times [OH^-(aq)]}{0.1} = 1.8 \times 10^{-5} \text{ mol dm}^{-3}$

$[OH^-(aq)]^2 = 0.1 \times 1.8 \times 10^{-5} \text{ mol}^2 \text{ dm}^{-6}$

$[OH^-(aq)] = \sqrt{1.8} \times 10^{-3} \text{ mol dm}^{-3}$ i.e. $1.34 \times 10^{-3} \text{ mol dm}^{-3}$

$pOH = 2.9$ so pH is $14 - 2.9 = 11.1$ *(2 marks)*

(c) (i) During the addition of the first 9 cm^3 of alkali, the pH of the ethanoic acid solution changes only gradually through the pH range of the methyl orange indicator. The solution would become yellow well before the 25 cm^3 equivalence point.   *(1 mark)*

During the titration of the hydrochloric acid, the pH of the solution stays below 3.1 until 24.5 cm^3 of alkali has been added. At the equivalence point, a few drops of alkali causes the pH to change sharply through the pH range of the indicator. So in this case the colour of the solution would change suddenly from pink through orange to yellow.   *(1 mark)*

(ii) A buffer solution. *(1 mark)*

The solution contains equal amounts of weak acid, $CH_3CO_2H(aq)$, and conjugate base, $CH_3CO_2^-(aq)$. It is at its maximum buffering point with a pH ($= pK_a$) of about 4.8 which would be unchanged by the addition of small amounts of acid or alkali. *(1 mark)*

(total 10 marks)

Question 3

(a) (i)
$$HInd(aq) \rightleftharpoons H^+(aq) + Ind^-(aq)$$

$$\frac{[H^+(aq)][Ind^-(aq)]}{[HInd(aq)]} = K_{ind}$$

Taking logarithms: $\log [H^+(aq)] + \log ([Ind^-(aq)]/[HInd(aq)]) = \log K_{ind}$

Hence: $-pH + \log ([Ind^-(aq)]/[HInd(aq)]) = -pK_{ind}$

Rearranging: $-pH = -pK_{ind} - \log ([Ind^-(aq)]/[HInd(aq)])$

Hence: $pH = pK_{ind} + \log ([Ind^-(aq)]/[HInd(aq)])$ *(3 marks)*

(ii) pH is 4.0 (because $[HInd(aq)] = [Ind^-(aq)]$ when equal intensities of yellow and blue give green mid-point colour). Then $\log ([Ind^-(aq)]/[HInd(aq)])$ is $\log 1 = 0$, so pH is $pK_{ind} = 4.0$) *(1 mark)*

(iii) Blue. In $0.1 \, mol \, dm^{-3}$ NaOH(aq) the pH = 13 (because pOH = 1 and pH is $14 - pOH$), so $13 = 7 + \log ([Ind^-(aq)]/[HInd(aq)])$. If $\log ([Ind^-(aq)]/[HInd(aq)]) = 6$, $[Ind^-(aq)] = 10^6 \times [HInd(aq)]$. *(2 marks)*

(b) (i) A solution of a weak acid and its conjugate base (or weak base and its conjugate acid) whose pH is almost unchanged by the addition of small amounts of acid or alkali. *(2 marks)*

(ii) In the buffer solution $CH_3CO_2H(aq) \rightleftharpoons H^+(aq) + CH_3CO_2^-(aq)$ and ethanoic acid molecules are in equilibrium with ethanoate ions. When acid is added, momentarily increasing the $[H^+(aq)]$, the conjugate base reacts with the added $H^+(aq)$ and the equilibrium shifts to the left. When alkali is added, momentarily increasing the $[OH^-(aq)]$, the acid reacts with the added $OH^-(aq)$ and the equilibrium shifts to the right. *(4 marks)*

Tip If the buffer contains ammonia and ammonium chloride, then $pOH = pK_b + \log ([NH_4^+(aq)]/[NH_3(aq)])$.

(iii) $pH = pK_a + \log ([CH_3CO_2^-(aq)]/[CH_3CO_2H(aq)])$
$= -\log (1.8 \times 10^{-5}) + \log (0.40 / 0.10)$
hence pH = 5.3   *(4 marks)*

(total 16 marks)

TOPIC 5   Electrochemistry and redox

Question 1

(a) (i) 1 atm *(1 mark)*

(ii) Platinum metal coated in platinum black (a catalyst of finely divided platinum) *(1 mark)*

(iii) Aqueous (hydrochloric) acid giving a concentration of $1 \, mol \, dm^{-3}$ $H_3O^+(aq)$ *(2 marks)*

Tip The Nernst equation gives a straight line $y = mx + c$, where the slope (m) is RT/nF and the intercept (c) on the y-axis is $E^\ominus$

(b) (i) 0.80 V *(1 mark)*

(ii) At 0.78 V the value of $\ln [Ag+(aq)] = -0.775$ so the concentration of silver ions would be $0.46 \, mol \, dm^{-3}$ *(2 marks)*

(iii) Slope (gradient) of graph is $RT/nF = (0.800 - 0.7730) / (0.0 - (-1.0)) \approx 0.027$ So $\{8.3 \, (J \, K^{-1} mol^{-1}) \times 298 \, (K)\}/(1 \times F) = 0.027$ (V or $J \, C^{-1}$) Hence value for F would be $8.3 \times 298/0.027 = 92\,000 \, C \, mol^{-1}$ *(2 marks)*

(total 9 marks)

Question 2

(a) The e.m.f. of an electrochemical cell under standard conditions of temperature (298 K), pressure (1 atm) and electrolyte concentration (1 mol dm^{-3}) represented by the cell diagram $Pt[H_2(g)]|2H^+(aq) \vdots\vdots M^{n+}(aq)|M(s)$, where M(s) and $M^{n+}(aq)$ represent the metal and its cations. *(2 marks)*

(b) The standard electrode potentials, $E^{\ominus}$, of zinc and copper are -0.76 V and $+0.34$ V respectively.

(i)

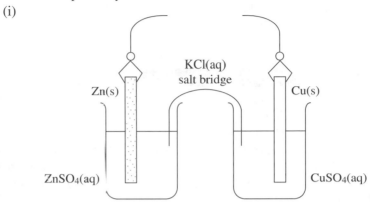

(2 marks)

(ii) E.m.f. is $(+0.34) - (-0.76) = +1.10$ V   *(1 mark)*

(iii) A very high internal resistance voltmeter   *(1 mark)*

(iv) From the zinc to the copper   *(1 mark)*

(v) $Zn(s) + Cu^{2+}(aq) \rightarrow Zn^{2+}(aq) + Cu(s)$ *(1 mark)*

redox potentials in ascending order

oxidising power	$\frac{1}{2}I_2 + e^- \leftrightharpoons I^-$	$+0.54$
	$Fe^{3+} + e^- \leftrightharpoons Fe^{2+}$	$+0.77$
	$Ag^+ + e^- \leftrightharpoons Ag$	$+0.80$
	$BrO_3^- + 6H^+ + 5e^- \leftrightharpoons \frac{1}{2}Br_2 + 3H_2O$	reducing power $+1.52$

Tip Note the connection between oxidizing and reducing powers.

(c) (i) Bromate(V) ions would oxidize iodide ions to iodine molecules and be reduced to bromine molecules: $BrO_3^- + 6H^+ + 5I^- \rightarrow \frac{1}{2}Br2 + 3H_2O + 2\frac{1}{2}I_2$ because the $E^{\ominus}$ for the acidified bromate is more positive than that for iodine. *(2 marks)*

(ii) No reaction because the $E^{\ominus}$ for silver ions is more positive than that for iron(III) ions. (Silver ions would oxidize iron(II) ions to iron(III) ions and be reduced to silver.) *(2 marks)*

(iii) iron(III) ions would oxidize iodide ions to iodine molecules and be reduced to iron(II) ions: $Fe^{3+} + I^- \rightarrow Fe^{2+} + \frac{1}{2}I_2$ because the $E^{\ominus}$ for iron(III) ions is more positive than that for iodine. *(2 marks)*

(total 14 marks)

Question 3

Tip The more positive the redox potential, the stronger the oxidizing power of the L.H.S. of the system and the weaker the reducing power of the R.H.S. of the system.

(a) The vanadium(II) ion, $V^{2+}(aq)$, because the $E^{\ominus}$ of -0.26 V means that the oxidation product, $V^{3+}(aq)$, is the weakest of the three oxidizing agents shown in the table. *(2 marks)*

(b) The vanadate(V) ion, $VO_2^+(aq)$, because the $E^{\ominus}$ of $+1.00$ V is the only one of the above three that is more positive than the $E^{\ominus}$ of $+0.54$ V for iodine. In the other two cases which are below $+0.54$ V in the table, iodine would oxidize the vanadium(II), $V^{2+}(aq)$, to vanadium(III), $V^{3+}(aq)$, and further to vanadate(IV), $VO^{2+}(aq)$. *(3 marks)*

Tip The more negative the redox potential, the stronger the reducing power of the R.H.S. of the system and the weaker the oxidizing power of the L.H.S. of the system.

(c) The $E^{\ominus}$ of -0.76 V makes zinc capable of reducing all the vanadium oxidation states to $+2$. So, zinc would first reduce the vanadate(V) to vanadate(IV). When that reduction is complete, the vanadate(IV) would be reduced to vanadium(III). The zinc would then reduce the vanadium(III) to vanadium(II). *(3 marks)*

(d) The sulphite would be oxidized to sulphate and the vanadate(V) ions would be reduced to vanadate(IV)

$$2VO_2^+(aq) + H_2SO_3(aq) \rightarrow 2VO^{2+}(aq) + SO_4^{2-}(aq) + H_2O(l)$$

The vanadate(IV) would then be reduced to vanadium(III)

$$2VO^{2+}(aq) + 4H^+(aq) + H_2SO_3(aq) \rightarrow 2V^{3+}(aq) + SO_4^{2-}(aq) + 3H_2O(l)$$

The reason is that the $E^{\ominus}$ of $+0.17\,V$ shows that as a reducing agent the aqueous sulphur dioxide is stronger than vanadate(IV) or vanadium(III) but weaker than vanadium(II). *(3 marks)*

(total 11 marks)

TOPIC 6   The Periodic Table

Question 1

Tip (a) (i) Ionic bonding: s-block metal gives electrons to hydrogen.

(a) (i) Na^+H^- *(1 mark)*

(ii) H—Cl because chlorine is more electronegative than hydrogen. *(2 marks)*

(iii) CH_4 because the electronegativities of carbon and hydrogen are similar and the tetrahedral shape of the molecule gives a net dipole moment = zero. *(2 marks)*

Tip (a) (ii) Single polar covalent bond: two atoms share ONE PAIR of electrons UNEQUALLY.

(iv) $Na^+H^-(s) + H_2O(l) \rightarrow Na^+(aq) + OH^-(aq) + H_2(g)$ *(2 marks)*

(b) statement: oxides of Na and Mg are basic, aluminium oxide is amphoteric and the oxides of Si, P, S and Cl are acidic *(1 mark)*

sodium oxide: $Na_2O(s) + H_2O(l) \rightarrow 2Na^+(aq) + 2OH^-(aq)$ *(1 mark)*

sulphur dioxide: $SO_2(g) + H_2O(l) \rightarrow H_2SO_3(aq)$ *(1 mark)*

(c) (i) the oxides change from acidic (CO_2, SiO_2) to amphoteric (SnO_2, PbO_2) and become oxidizing agents (SnO_2, PbO_2) *(2 marks)*

(ii) from CCl_4 to $PbCl_4$ the chlorides show a decrease in thermal stability and an increase in the tendency to disproportionate into the divalent state, giving off chlorine gas *(2 marks)*

(d) Sodium chloride simply dissolves in water. Aluminium chloride fumes in moist air and dissolves exothermically in water to give an acidic solution. Silicon tetrachloride reacts violently with water to give dense fumes of hydrogen chloride and a gelatinous precipitate of hydrated silicon oxide (silica gel). *(3 marks)*

(e) There are similarities in the properties of the elements and their compounds not shared by the other elements in their groups. The chlorides form hydrated crystalline salts which are deliquescent and which hydrolyse on heating. *(3 marks)*

(total 20 marks)

Question 2

(a) Sulphates become less soluble with increasing atomic number because the cation becomes less hydrated as its size increases (and its charge density and polarizing power decrease) so the hydration enthalpy cannot compensate for the lattice enthalpy. *(2 marks)*

Tip You OBSERVE colours, smells, sounds, changes of state and temperature, formation of gases and precipitates. This is what the examiner wants to read.

(b) The colourless/white crystals of potassium nitrate would melt, give off a colourless gas and turn pale yellow/green *(2 marks)*

The colourless/white crystals of magnesium nitrate would melt, give off a brown, sharp-smelling (toxic) gas and eventually resolidify, melting into the glass of the tube. *(2 marks)*

(c) (i) The lithium ion is extremely small so that its charge density is much higher than that of the other alkali metal cations. Consequently the lithium cation so strongly attracts a polar water molecule that it can hold the molecule in a crystal lattice of the hydrated chloride. *(2 marks)*

(ii) The double positive charge makes the magnesium ion more strongly polarizing than the singly charged sodium ion. Consequently the Mg^{2+} ion distorts the much larger, polarizable carbonate anion and removes an oxygen to form MgO and release a carbon dioxide molecule. *(2 marks)*

(d) (i) The carbonate ion acts as a strong base and lowers the ratio of the concentration of the hydrogen ion to that of the hydroxide ion present in the water. $CO_3^{2-}(aq) + H_2O(l) \rightarrow HCO_3^-(aq) + OH^-(aq)$ *(2 marks)*

  (ii) The rain water contains aqueous carbon dioxide (orthocarbonic acid, H_2CO_3) which reacts with the limestone which is mainly calcium carbonate
$CaCO_3(s) + H_2O(l) + CO_2(aq) \rightarrow Ca^{2+}(aq) + 2HCO_3^-(aq)$ *(2 marks)*

(total 14 marks)

Question 3

(a) (i) $2Al(s) + Fe_2O_3(s) \rightarrow 2Fe(s) + Al_2O_3(s)$ *(1 mark)*

  (ii) $(-1669) - (-822) = -847\,kJ\,mol^{-1}$ *(1 mark)*

  (iii) An extremely thin but very tough layer of oxide adheres strongly to the aluminium surface and protects the underlying metal from attack. *(1 mark)*

Tip According to the Bronsted-Lowry theory, the $[Al(H_2O)_6]^{3+}$ ion, by donating a proton, is acting as an acid, and a solvent (water) molecule, by accepting a proton, is acting as a base.

(b) (i) The aqueous aluminium ion can donate protons and make the concentration of hydronium ions in the water greater than that of the hydroxide ions.

$[Al(H_2O)_6]^{3+}(aq) + H_2O \rightleftharpoons [Al(OH)(H_2O)_5]^{2+}(aq) + H_3O^+(aq)$ *(2 marks)*

  (ii) When the colourless solutions are mixed, a colourless gas is given off (which turns limewater milky) and a white gelatinous precipitate is formed.

$2[Al(H_2O)_6]^{3+}(aq) + 3CO_3^{2-}(aq) \rightarrow 2Al(OH)_3(s) + 3CO_2(g) + 9H_2O(l)$
(2 marks)

  (iii) The aqueous alkali removes protons from the hydrated aluminium cation to form a gelatinous white precipitate of aluminium hydroxide which then dissolves in excess alkali to form an aqueous hydroxyaluminate.

$[Al(H_2O)_6]^{3-}(aq) + 3OH^-(aq) \rightarrow Al[(H_2O)_3(OH)_3](s) + 3H_2O(l)$

$Al[(H_2O)_3(OH)_3](s) + 3OH^-(aq) \rightarrow [Al(OH)_6]^{3-}(aq) + 6H_2O(l)$ *(4 marks)*

(c) (i) AlF_6^{3-} *(1 mark)*

  (ii) As a 'solvent' (for bauxite) or flux (to lower the melting point of aluminium oxide) in the industrial extraction of aluminium by electrolysis. *(1 mark)*

(d) (i) BH_4^- *(1 mark)*

  (ii) As a reducing agent in organic chemistry to convert carboxylic acids, ketones and aldehydes into alcohols. *(1 mark)*

(total 15 marks)

Question 4

(a) (i) SiO_2 *(1 mark)* (ii) PbO *(1 mark)* (iii) PbO_2 *(1 mark)* (iv) CO *(1 mark)*

Tip $PbO_2 + 4HCl \rightarrow PbCl_2 + 2H_2O + Cl_2$ where the oxidation state of Pb goes from $+4$ to $+2$ and that of Cl goes from -1 to 0.

(b) (i) Silicon tetrachloride reacts vigorously with cold water to give off steamy fumes of hydrogen chloride and form a hot gel of hydrated silicon oxide

$SiCl_4(l) + 2H_2O(l) \rightarrow SiO_2(s) + 4HCl(g)$.

The silicon atom can extend its outer electron shell beyond 8, so it is open to nucleophilic attack by a water molecule whose oxygen atom can use one of its lone pairs of electrons to form a dative bond. Cold water does not react with tetrachloromethane because the central carbon atom cannot extend its outer electron shell beyond 8 and the C—Cl is difficult to break. *(3 marks)*

  (ii) The Group 4 elements have four electrons in their outer shell and consequently an oxidation number of $+4$. With increasing atomic number down the Group, there is an increasing tendency for the elements to form stable compounds in which the oxidation number is $+2$. This tendency for two of the four valence electrons not to participate in bonding as atomic number increases is known as the inert pair effect. It is related to the trends in bond, ionization and lattice energies. *(3 marks)*

  (iii) $PbCl_4(l) + 2H_2O(l) \rightarrow PbO_2(s) + 4HCl(g)$ *(1 mark)*

(c) (i) Increasing the concentration of the HCl(aq) prevents the formation of the insoluble basic tin chloride by forming tin-chlorocomplexes and causing a shift in the equilibrium $SnCl_2(s) + H_2O(l) \rightleftharpoons Sn(OH)Cl(s) + HCl(aq)$ from right to left. *(2 marks)*

(ii) $SnCl_2(aq) + 2FeCl_3(aq) \rightarrow SnCl_4(aq) + 2FeCl_2(aq)$ *(1 mark)*

(iii) The metallic tin would prevent the formation of any tin(IV) chloride by atmospheric oxygen dissolved in the water.

$Sn(s) + SnCl_4(aq) \rightarrow 2SnCl_2(aq)$ *(1 mark)*

(total 15 marks)

Question 5

(a) sodium chloride: A colourless, sharp-smelling gas is given off which forms steamy fumes in moist air. *(1 mark)*

sodium bromide: The colourless mixture turns to a brown liquid and a gas, with a choking smell and a colour varying from pale yellow to dark red-brown, is given off which forms steamy fumes in moist air. *(2 marks)*

sodium iodide: The colourless mixture turns to a dark brown liquid and a grey metallic-like solid higher in the tube. A gas with a bad-egg smell is given off together with a purple vapour and a gas which forms steamy fumes in moist air. *(2 marks)*

(b) (i) Redox (reduction/oxidation) *(1 mark)*

Tip The names of the anions composed of more than one element end with *ate*: e.g. HSO_4^- is hydrogensulphate, MnO_4^- is manganate(VII) and $CuCl_4^{2-}$ is tetrachlorocuprate(II).

(ii) ClO^- = chlorate(I) (hypochlorite); ClO_3^- = chlorate(V) *(2 marks)*

(iii) NaClO sterilizing and bleaching agent. *(1 mark)*
$NaClO_3$ weed-killer *(1 mark)*

(c) (i) Hydrogen fluoride gives a weak dimeric acid in aqueous solution but the other hydrogen halides give strong monomeric acids.

$H_2F_2(aq) \rightleftharpoons H^+(aq) + HF_2^-(aq)$ *(1 mark)*

(ii) Silver fluoride is soluble in water but the other silver halides are sparingly soluble salts becoming progressively less soluble from AgCl to AgI. *(1 mark)*

(total 12 marks)

Question 6

Tip Look at question (a)(ii) and you have a strong clue to the answer for (a)(i).

(a) (i) Zn $1s^2 2s^2 2p^6 3s^2 3p^6 3d^{10} 4s^2$ The element is atypical because it retains a complete set of d-electrons and exists in only the one oxidation state of $+2$ (other than zero when uncombined). *(2 marks)*

(ii) $(+2)$ V^{2+} $(+3)$ V^{3+} $(+4)$ VO^{2+} $(+5)$ VO_2^+ *(4 marks)*

(iii) hard metals with high melting and boiling points
metals and their compounds are good catalysts
form highly coloured compounds
form complexes by acting as Lewis acids *(4 marks)*

(b) (i) $Cr_2O_7^{2-}(aq) + 14H^+(aq) + 6e^- \rightarrow 2Cr^{3+}(aq) + 7H_2O(aq)$ *(1 mark)*

(ii) $Cr_2O_7^{2-}(aq) + 14H^+(aq) + 6Fe^{2+}(aq) \rightarrow 2Cr^{3+}(aq) + 7H_2O(aq) + 6Fe^{3+}(aq)$ *(1 mark)*

(c) 1 mol $Cr_2O_7^{2-}(aq)$ oxidizes 6 mol $Fe^{2+}(aq)$
$30\,cm^3$ of $Cr_2O_7^{2-}(aq)$ of concentration $0.02\,mol\,dm^{-3}$ contain $0.02 \times 30/1000$
$= 6 \times 10^{-4}\,mol$ $Cr_2O_7^{2-}(aq)$ so the $25\,cm^3$ of aqueous iron(II) sulphate must contain $6 \times 6 \times 10^{-4}\,mol$ $Fe^{2+}(aq)$.
Hence the concentration is $6 \times 6 \times 10^{-4} \times 1000/25$
$= 0.14(4)\,mol\,dm^{-3}$ $Fe^{2+}(aq)$. *(2 marks)*

(total 14 marks)

TOPIC 7 Organic chemistry

Question 1

(a)(i) *cis*-but-2-ene   *trans*-but-2-ene

(2 marks)

Tip No free rotation about a carbon–carbon double bond is one reason for geometrical isomerism. Remember inorganic geometric isomers also exist.

(ii) The methyl groups are further apart in the *trans*-isomer than in the *cis*-isomer, so the repulsion (or steric hindrance) between the two groups is less in the *trans*-isomer which therefore would be expected to be more stable energetically than the *cis*-isomer.   *(2 marks)*

(b) (i) homolytic fission   *(1 mark)*

(ii) radical (or free radical)   *(1 mark)*

(iii)

$$CH_3 \quad CH_3 \qquad\qquad CH_3 \quad H$$
$$I-C-C\cdot \quad\longrightarrow\quad C=C \quad + \; I\cdot$$
$$H \qquad H \qquad\qquad H \qquad CH_3$$

(2 marks)

(iv) Rotation can occur about the single bond joining carbon atoms 2 and 3.   *(1 mark)*

(c) (i) *cis*-butenedioic acid would form the anhydride because the two carboxyl groups are close enough together. They are too far apart in trans-butenedioic acid.

$$\text{(diagram of cis-butenedioic acid} \longrightarrow \text{anhydride)}$$

(2 marks)

(ii) Hydrogen reduces the double bond to a single bond which allows free rotation, so geometric isomers are no longer possible.

$$\text{(diagram)} \xrightarrow{H_2} \text{(diagram)}$$

(2 marks)

Hydrogen bromide adds across the double bond to give molecules with a chiral centre (*), so optical isomers are possible.

$$\text{(diagram)} \xrightarrow{HBr} \text{(diagram with } C^* \text{)}$$

(2 marks)

(total 15 marks)

Question 2

Tip According to the Lewis acid–base theory, an electrophile, by accepting an electron pair, is acting as an acid and a nucleophile, by donating an electron pair, is acting as a base.

(a) A nucleophile provides a pair of electrons to form a dative bond.   *(1 mark)*

An electrophile accepts a pair of electrons to form a dative bond.   *(1 mark)*

(b)(i)

$$HO\colon^- \quad \begin{array}{c} H \\ | \\ C-Br \\ | \\ H\, C_3H_7 \end{array} \longrightarrow HO-\begin{array}{c} H \\ | \\ C \diagdown H \\ | \\ C_3H_7 \end{array} + \; Br^-$$

(3 marks)

(ii) The reaction is found to be second order overall, being first order with respect to the concentration of both the hydroxide ion and the bromobutane molecule.   *(2 marks)*

(c) Warm one drop of the liquid with aqueous sodium hydroxide then acidify with aqueous nitric acid and add aqueous silver nitrate to the acidic solution. The 1-bromobutane would give an off-white or very pale yellow precipitate (of silver bromide). Bromobenzene would not react. *(4 marks)*

(d) (i) A radical is an atom, uncombined or in a group, with an unpaired electron (represented by ·): e.g. a chlorine radical is an uncombined atom $:\ddot{\text{C}}\text{l}\cdot$

(1 mark)

A CFC is a chlorofluoromethane such as CCl_2F_2 and CCl_3F. *(1 mark)*

(ii) $CCl_2F_2 \rightarrow \cdot CClF_2 + Cl\cdot$ *(1 mark)*

(iii) $2O_3 \rightarrow 3O_2$ *(1 mark)*

(iv) The chlorine radical acts as a catalyst because it takes part in the reaction but is not used up. *(2 marks)*

(total 17 marks)

Question 3

(a) (i) Aldehyde (ii) Ketone (iii) Carboxyl (iv) Secondary alcohol:

(4 marks)

(b) (i) Add a small piece of sodium metal to each liquid. The ethanol reacts vigorously to give off a colourless gas which can be collected over water, mixed with air and ignited to produce a loud 'pop'.

$C_2H_5OH + Na \rightarrow C_2H_5O^-Na^+ + \frac{1}{2}H_2$. Dry propanone does not react.

(2 marks)

(ii) Warm a few drops of the liquid with Fehling's solution (an aqueous alkaline solution made with copper(II) sulphate, sodium 2,3-dihydroxybutanedioate and sodium hydroxide). The propanal is oxidized to propanoic acid and an orange-red precipitate of copper(I) oxide forms. Propanone does not react.

$C_2H_5CHO + 2Cu^{2+} + 4OH^- \rightarrow C_2H_5CO_2H + Cu_2O + 2H_2O$ *(2 marks)*

(iii) Warm a few drops of the liquid with a mixture of iodine and aqueous sodium hydroxide for a few minutes then allow the resulting solution to cool. The propan-2-ol yields a pale-yellow crystalline precipitate of triiodomethane (iodoform).

$(CH_3)_2CH(OH) + 3I_2 + 4OH^- \rightarrow CHI_3 + CH_3CO_2^- + 3I^- + 2H_2O$

The propan-1-ol does not react. *(2 marks)*

(iv) Dissolve a small sample in warm water and then add aqueous sodium carbonate. The benzoic acid solution will fizz and give off a colourless gas which turns limewater milky. The phenol solution does not react.

$2C_6H_5CO_2H + Na_2CO_3 \rightarrow 2C_6H_5CO_2Na + H_2O + CO_2$ *(2 marks)*

Tip Sulphuric acid is a homogeneous catalyst when forming esters from carboxylic acids and alcohols. The mechanism involves proton transfer.

(c) (i) Heat under reflux with an acid catalyst *(2 marks)*

(ii) $CH_3CO_2H + C_2H_5OH \rightleftharpoons CH_3CO_2C_2H_5 + H_2O$ *(1 mark)*

(iii) $CH_3COCl + C_2H_5OH \rightarrow CH_3CO_2C_2H_5 + HCl$ *(1 mark)*

(iv)

(1 mark)

(total 17 marks)

Question 4

(a) primary   secondary   tertiary

$$CH_3-N\begin{smallmatrix}H\\[2pt]\\[2pt]H\end{smallmatrix} \qquad CH_3-N\begin{smallmatrix}H\\[2pt]\\[2pt]CH_3\end{smallmatrix} \qquad CH_3-N\begin{smallmatrix}CH_3\\[2pt]\\[2pt]CH_3\end{smallmatrix}$$

(3 marks)

(b) (i) An off-white or very pale yellow precipitate (of silver bromide).   *(1 mark)*

    (ii) $CH_3CH_2CH_2CH_2C_2H_2CH_2CH_2CH_2CH_2CH_2CH_2CH_2CH_2CH_2CH_2CH_2Br$

       or $CH_3(CH_2)_{14}CH_2Br$ *(1 mark)*

    (iii) $N(CH_3)_3 + CH_3(CH_2)_{14}CH_2Br \rightarrow CH_3(CH_2)_{14}CH_2N(CH_3)_3Br$ *(1 mark)*

(c) (i)

$$\underset{\substack{|\\CH_3-CH_2-CH-CH_2-CH_3}}{NH_2} \xrightarrow{HNO_2} \underset{\substack{|\\CH_3-CH_2-CH-CH_2-CH_3}}{OH} + N_2 + H_2O$$

(1 mark)

Tip With nitrous acid, aromatic amines give nitrogen quantitatively on heating but at low temperature can be diazotized to make dyes. Aliphatic diazonium ions are unstable even at low temperature and evolve nitrogen immediately.

    (ii) molar mass of 3-aminopentane is

         $(5 \times 12) + (13 \times 1) + (1 \times 14) = 87\,g\,mol^{-1}$.

         so 8.7 g is 0.1 mole of 3-aminopentane.

         1 mol 3-aminopentane yields 1 mol N_2 gas = 22.4 dm^3 at s.t.p.

         so volume of nitrogen obtained would be 2.24 dm^3 at s.t.p.   *(2 marks)*

(d)   benzylamine   ethylmethylamine

     or phenylmethylamine

$$ \text{—}CH_2\text{—}NH_2 \qquad\qquad CH_3\text{—}CH_2\text{—}N\begin{smallmatrix}H\\[2pt]\\[2pt]CH_3\end{smallmatrix}$$

(4 marks)

(total 13 marks)

Question 5

(a) (i) name: Friedel-Crafts reaction

         type of reaction: electrophilic substitution   *(2 marks)*

    (ii) **I** propene   **III** phenol

         II (1-methylethyl)benzene or 2-phenylpropane   **IV** propanone   *(4 marks)*

    (iii) crude petroleum oil   *(1 mark)*

Tip (b) (i) A substituted benzene compound forms mainly 1,2- and 1,4- substitution products if the group already attached to the ring is electron-donating: e.g. $-CH_3$, $-OH$ and $-NH_2$.

Tip (b) (ii) A substituted benzene compound forms mainly 1,3- substitution products if the group already attached to the ring is electron-attracting: e.g. $-CO_2H$, $-NO_2$ and $-SO_3H$.

(b)(i)

$$O^-Na^+$$

(ii)

Br—(OH)—Br with Br

(2 marks)

(total 9 marks)

Question 6

(a) (i) To start the polymerization by providing free radicals

         $(^-O_3SO-OSO_3^- \rightarrow 2O_3SO\cdot)$ *(1 mark)*

    (ii)

$$\underset{F}{\overset{F}{C}}=\underset{F}{\overset{F}{C}} \qquad -\overset{F}{\underset{F}{C}}-\overset{F}{\underset{F}{C}}-\overset{F}{\underset{F}{C}}-\overset{F}{\underset{F}{C}}-\overset{F}{\underset{F}{C}}-\overset{F}{\underset{F}{C}}-$$

(2 marks)

    (iii) Used where insulation, non-stick and protective surfaces are needed. Polymer has a very high electrical resistivity and a very low frictional coefficient.

(2 marks)

(b) (i)   ethane-1,2-diol   benzene-1,4-dicarboxylic acid

$$\underset{\substack{|\;\;|\;\;|\\H\;\;H\;\;H}}{\overset{\substack{H\;\;H\;\;H\\|\;\;|\;\;|}}{O-C-C-O}} \qquad\qquad H-O{\overset{\diagup}{\underset{\diagdown}{}}}\overset{O}{\underset{}{C}}-(\bigcirc)-\overset{O}{\underset{}{C}}{\overset{\diagup}{\underset{\diagdown}{}}}O-H$$

(3 marks)

(ii)

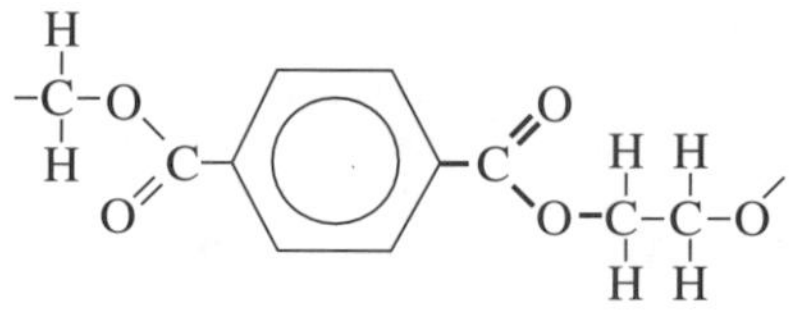

or

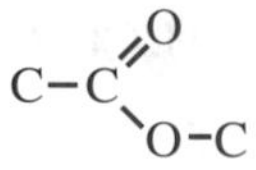

(1 mark)

Tip The simpler drawing is all you would need but you would not get the mark for this:

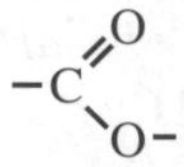

Can you see why?

(iii)

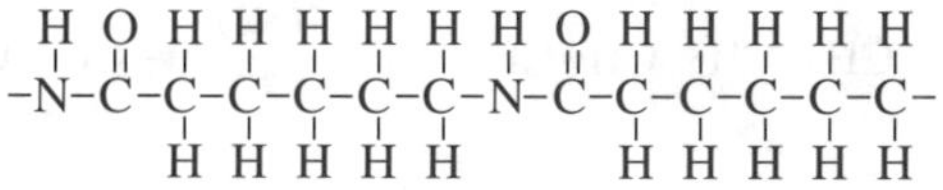

(2 marks)

(iv) Polyester fibres for production of cloth and fabrics. Nylons for production of high tensile strength ropes and low-friction moulded components. *(2 marks)*

(total 13 marks)

part IV
Practice papers, answers and mark schemes

Timed practice papers

PRACTICE PAPER 1 (1½ hr) General chemistry

Question 1

(a) When aqueous barium chloride is added to an aqueous solution, **A**, a white precipitate is observed.
  (i) Write down the formulae of **two** anions which could be present in **A** if the solution is not acidic. (2 marks)
  (ii) Write down the formula of **one** anion which could be present in **A** if the solution is acidic. (1 mark)

(b) When aqueous sodium hydroxide is added to an aqueous solution, **B**, a white precipitate is observed. When excess aqueous sodium hydroxide is added, the precipitate disappears to leave a colourless solution. Write down the formulae of **two** cations which could be present in **B**. (2 marks)

(c) Describe what would be observed if each of the following were added to aqueous potassium iodide. Write balanced equations for any reactions which occur.
  (i) Aqueous copper(II) sulphate (3 marks)
  (ii) Acidified aqueous potassium manganate(VII) (3 marks)

(d) Describe what would be observed if each of the following were added to acidified aqueous iron(II) sulphate. Write equations for any reactions which occur.
  (i) Aqueous ammonia (2 marks)
  (ii) Aqueous potassium manganate(VII) (2 marks)

(e) 21.5 cm^3 of aqueous sodium thiosulphate of concentration 0.0105 mol dm^{-3} $S_2O_3^{2-}$(aq) were required to titrate 25.0 cm^3 of aqueous iodine I_2(aq).
  (i) Write a balanced equation for the reaction of aqueous sodium thiosulphate with aqueous iodine. (2 marks)
  (ii) Calculate the concentration of the aqueous iodine. (2 marks)

(total 19 marks)

Question 2

(a) There are three kinds of metal crystal structure. Most metals have one or other of the two close-packed structures but alkali metals have body-centred structures.
  (i) Give the names of the two close-packed metal structures. (2 marks)
  (ii) What is meant by the term *coordination number* and what is its value in a close-packed metallic crystal structure? (2 marks)
  (iii) Draw a diagram to show the arrangement of atoms in a body-centred cubic structure and state the value of the coordination number. (2 marks)

(b) Some molten metals do not mix with each other but molten transition elements readily form uniform solutions which solidify to produce alloys.
  (i) Suggest a reason why the molten transition elements readily mix to form alloys. (1 mark)
  (ii) Name two transition elements of the 3d series that form the components of an alloy and give the name of the alloy. (3 marks)
  (iii) State and explain an important use for the alloy in (ii) above. (2 marks)

(c) Many of the transition metals can combine with small non-metallic atoms to form non-stoichiometric interstitial compounds.
  (i) What is meant by the term *non-stoichiometric*? (1 mark)
  (ii) What is meant by the term *interstitial compound*? (2 marks)

(total 15 marks)

Question 3

(a) State **three** different physical methods for following the rates of chemical reactions. (3 marks)

(b) The rate equation for the alkaline hydrolysis of 2-bromo-2-methylpropane is

$$rate = k[(CH_3)_3CBr]$$

(i) What is the order of this reaction? (1 mark)

(ii) Write an equation for the rate-determining step of the reaction. (1 mark)

(iii) Why would you expect the subsequent step of the mechanism to be a fast reaction? (1 mark)

(c) The reaction $H_2O_2(aq) + 2H^+(aq) + 2I^-(aq) \rightarrow I_2(aq) + 2H_2O(l)$
can be followed using the iodine clock technique described below.

> The concentration of the reactant being studied is made very much smaller than the concentrations of the other two reactants. Starch indicator and a small but constant amount of sodium thiosulphate are added to each reaction mixture. During the reaction, aqueous thiosulphate ions reduce any iodine molecules back to aqueous iodide ions. The blue colour of a starch-iodine complex only appears at some time (t) after the start of the reaction when all the sodium thiosulphate has been used up.

(i) What could serve as a measure of the initial rate of reaction? (1 mark)

(ii) Why should the concentration of the reactant being studied be made much smaller than the concentrations of the other two reactants? (1 mark)

(iii) If the reaction is first order with respect to $H_2O_2(aq)$, first order with respect to $I^-(aq)$ and second order overall, write an expression for the rate equation. (2 marks)

(iv) What would be the effect upon the rate of the reaction of doubling the concentration of all three reactants? (2 marks)

(total 12 marks)

Question 4

(a) Outline briefly how you would attempt to measure the equilibrium constant value at 323 K for the hydrolysis of ethyl ethanoate.

$$CH_3CO_2C_2H_5(l) + H_2O(l) \rightleftharpoons CH_3CO_2H(l) + C_2H_5OH(l)$$ (5 marks)

(b) When 2 mol of ethanoic acid are mixed with 1 mol of ethanol at 298 K and the mixture allowed to reach equilibrium, 0.845 mol of the ester forms. Calculate the value of the equilibrium constant, K_c, for the esterification reaction

$$CH_3CO_2H(l) + C_2H_5OH(l) \rightleftharpoons CH_3CO_2C_2H_5(l) + H_2O(l)$$ (4 marks)

(c) Carbon monoxide can be removed from gaseous mixtures by converting it into carbon dioxide which could then be dissolved in water. This method depends upon the exothermic reaction $CO(g) + H_2O(g) \rightleftharpoons CO_2(g) + H_2(g)$
for which the value of the standard Gibb's free energy change, $\Delta G^\ominus$, at 800 K, is -8.27 kJ mol^{-1}.

(i) What might be the advantages or disadvantages of using a high pressure? (2 marks)

(ii) What might be the advantages or disadvantages of using a temperature lower than 800 K (2 marks)

(iii) Use the relationship $\Delta G^\ominus = -RT \ln K_p$ to calculate the value of K_p at 800 K. $(R = 8.31\,J\,K^{-1}\,mol^{-1})$ (2 marks)

(total 15 marks)

Question 5

This question concerns aqueous ions of chromium in which the element has stable oxidation states: $+2$, $+3$ and $+6$.

$$Cr^{3+}(aq) + e^- \rightleftharpoons Cr^{2+}(aq) \qquad\qquad E^\ominus = -0.41\,V$$

$$Cr_2O_7^{2-}(aq) + 14H^+(aq) + 6e^- \rightleftharpoons 2Cr^{3+}(aq) + 7H_2O(l) \quad E^\ominus = +1.33\,V$$

$$O_2(g) + 4H^+(aq) + 4e^- \rightleftharpoons 2H_2O(l) \qquad\qquad E^\ominus = +1.23\,V$$

$$Zn^{2+}(aq) + 2e^- \rightleftharpoons Zn(s) \qquad\qquad E^\ominus = -0.76\,V$$

(a) (i) Which ion of chromium is the strongest reducing ion? (1 mark)
  (ii) Use the $Cr^{3+}(aq)/Cr^{2+}(aq)$ system to complete the following cell diagram.
    $Pt\,|\,[2Cr^{3+}(aq) + 7H_2O(l)],[Cr_2O_7^{2-}(aq) + 14H^+(aq)]\,\vdots$ (1 mark)

  (iii) What would be the standard e.m.f. of the above electrochemical cell and
    which electrode would be positive? (1 mark)
  (iv) Write a balanced equation for the overall reaction that would occur if the
    terminals of the electrochemical cell were connected by a metal wire.
                                                                              (1 mark)
  (v) Explain why zinc can be used to prepare aqueous chromium(II) ions from
    chromium(III) ions. (1 mark)
  (vi) Write a balanced equation for the reaction of aqueous dichromate(VI)
    ions with an excess of zinc metal. (1 mark)
  (vii) State and explain what practical precaution should be taken in the
    preparation of chromium(II) compounds. (2 marks)
(b) (i) Write down the formula of the chromate(VI) ion. (1 mark)
  (ii) In aqueous solution, chromate(VI) ions are in equilibrium with
    dichromate(VI) ions. Write an equation for this equilibrium. (2 marks)
  (iii) State and explain what is observed when dilute acid is added to aqueous
    potassium chromate(VI). (2 marks)
  (iv) Explain why a yellow precipitate of barium chromate(VI) is obtained
    when aqueous barium chloride is added to aqueous potassium
    dichromate(VI). (2 marks)
                                                                   (total 15 marks)

Question 6

In the UK one of the main fuels was *coal-gas* until it was replaced in the 1960s by *natural gas*. Coal-gas was manufactured by destructive distillation: heating coal in the absence of air. The following table shows a typical composition of coal gas.

constituent	hydrogen	methane	carbon monoxide	ethene	nitrogen
% by volume:	50	32	8	4	6

(a) (i) Explain why destructive distillation was performed in the absence of air.
                                                                              (1 mark)
  (ii) Give the name of the main constituent of natural gas. (1 mark)
  (iii) State **two** advantages, other than economic, of natural gas over coal-gas
    as a fuel. (2 marks)
  (iv) Calculate the average molar mass of coal-gas.

    $(A_r(H) = 1.008; A_r(C)\ 12.01; A_r(N) = 14.01; A_r(O) = 16.00)$ (2 marks)

  (v) Use your answer from (iv) to calculate the density of coal gas at 25.0 °C
    and 1 atm. (Molar volume $= 22.4\ dm^3$ at 0 °C and 1 atm.) (2 marks)
(b) Metal hydrides may provide a convenient means of storing hydrogen for use as a
  fuel. Calcium hydride is prepared by heating the metal in a stream of the *dry* gas.
  (i) Write an equation for the combination of calcium and hydrogen to form
    calcium hydride. (1 mark)

(ii) Write down the formula to show the bonding present in calcium hydride.

(1 mark)

(iii) Write an equation for the reaction of excess water with calcium hydride.

(1 mark)

(iv) Compare the reaction in (b)(i) with the reaction in (b)(iii) and comment on the possible use of calcium as a means of storing hydrogen.   (2 marks)

(v) Suggest one reason, other than economic, why hydrogen has not replaced natural gas as the main fuel in the UK.   (1 mark)

(total 14 marks)

Total mark for the paper: 90

PRACTICE PAPER 2 (1¼ hr) Inorganic chemistry

Question 1

(a) The atomic numbers of copper, iron and scandium are 29, 26 and 21 respectively. The ground state electronic configuration of scandium may be represented as follows: Sc [argon core] 3d [↑][ ][ ][ ][ ] 4s [↑↓]. Using the same convention of arrows in boxes, give the ground state electronic configuration of

(i) Cu, Fe^{2+} and Fe^{3+}.   (3 marks)

(ii) Comment upon the relative stabilities of the iron(II) and iron(III) ions.

(2 marks)

(b) In Group 2 of the Periodic Table the radii of the cations increase with increasing atomic number. State, giving your reasons, the effect of this trend in ionic radius on

(i) the lattice enthalpies of the Group 2 chlorides   (2 marks)

(ii) the hydration enthalpies of the cations   (2 marks)

(iii) the solubilities of the Group 2 sulphates   (2 marks)

(c) Boron nitride, BN, is a slippery white solid with a layer structure similar to that of graphite.

(i) Write down the ground state electronic structures of boron and nitrogen in terms of s and p electrons.   (2 marks)

(ii) Draw a sketch to show the likely arrangement of boron and nitrogen atoms in a layer of a boron nitride crystal.   (2 marks)

(total 15 marks)

Question 2

(a) Explain why nitrogen only forms the trichloride, NCl_3, whereas phosphorus is able to form both a trichloride, PCl_3 and a pentachloride, PCl_5.   (2 marks)

(b) Draw the structures of the species present in phosphorus pentachloride (i) in the vapour phase and (ii) in the solid phase.   (3 marks)

(c) A total of 50 cm^3 of aqueous sodium hydroxide of concentration 0.1 mol dm^{-3} is added from a burette to 10 cm^3 of aqueous phosphoric acid, H_3PO_4, of concentration 0.1 mol dm^{-3} in a conical flask.

Draw a sketch to show how the pH of the solution in the flask varies with the volume of alkali added. Insert suitable numerical values for the pH (on the y-axis) and the volume of alkali added (on the x-axis).   (4 marks)

(d) For the Group 5 trihydrides NH_3, PH_3, AsH_3 and SbH_3, comment on any similarities or trends in **each** of the following.

(i) The shape of the molecules   (2 marks)

(ii) The bond angles   (2 marks)

(iii) Their basic nature   (2 marks)

(iv) Their thermal stabilities   (2 marks)

(total 17 marks)

Question 3

(a) Oxides of nitrogen are emitted in the exhaust fumes of motor cars and cause poor air quality in the inner cities. The molecular formulae of four oxides of nitrogen are N_2O, NO, NO_2 and N_2O_4.

    (i) Draw structures for N_2O and N_2O_4.   (2 marks)

    (ii) Explain why NO and NO_2 are able to take part in free radical reactions.

                                                                      (2 marks)

    (iii) Write a balanced equation for the reaction of NO_2 with aqueous sodium hydroxide and give the name for this type of reaction.   (2 marks)

(b) By writing equations and naming the relevant products, show how the thermal decomposition of potassium nitrate differs from that of copper(II) nitrate.

                                                                       (4 marks)

(c) Hydrazine, N_2H_4, is a weak base and powerful reducing agent. Liquid hydrazine has been used as a rocket fuel with liquid dinitrogen tetraoxide as the oxidant. The products of the reaction are nitrogen and steam.

    (i) What is the oxidation number of nitrogen in hydrazine?   (1 mark)

    (ii) Draw a dot and cross diagram of the hydrazine molecule.   (1 mark)

    (iii) Suggest an explanation for the fact that the boiling points (in kelvin) of hydrazine, ammonia (NH_3) and phosphine (PH_3) are 387, 240 and 185 respectively.   (3 marks)

    (iv) Account for the fact that $10\ cm^3$ of a $0.1\ mol\ dm^{-3}\ N_2H_4(aq)$ will react with $10\ cm^3$ of a $0.1\ mol\ dm^{-3}\ H_2SO_4(aq)$ or $20\ cm^3$ of a $0.1\ mol\ dm^{-3}\ HCl(aq)$.   (2 marks)

    (v) Write a balanced equation for the reaction of hydrazine with dinitrogen tetraoxide.   (1 mark)

                                                                       (total 18 marks)

Question 4

(a) Phosphorus trichloride reacts with water to form phosphonic acid, H_3PO_3. One mole of the acid reacts with one mole of aqueous copper(II) ions to form one mole of copper atoms and one mole of phosphoric acid, H_3PO_4. Phosphonic acid is dibasic, forming only two salts with sodium hydroxide.

    (i) Write an equation for the reaction of phosphorus trichloride with water.

                                                                        (1 mark)

    (ii) Give the formulae of the two sodium salts of phosphonic acid.   (1 mark)

    (iii) Write an balanced equation for the reaction of phosphonic acid with aqueous copper(II) ions.   (2 marks)

    (iv) Draw a structural formula for the phosphonic acid molecule.   (1 mark)

(b) $150\ cm^3$ of aqueous sodium hydroxide of concentration $2.0\ mol\ dm^{-3}$ was added to $15\ g$ of a fertilizer containing ammonium sulphate and the mixture heated until ammonia was no longer evolved. $100\ cm^3$ of hydrochloric acid of concentration $1.0\ mol\ dm^{-3}$ were required to neutralize the unreacted sodium hydroxide. Determine the percentage by mass of ammonium sulphate in the fertilizer. $(A_r(H) = 1.0; A_r(N) = 14.0; A_r(O) = 16.00; A_r(S) = 32.0)$ (4 marks)

                                                                       (total 9 marks)

Question 5

(a) Write down the ground state electronic configurations, in terms of s, p and d electrons, of

    (i) a copper atom

    (ii) a copper(II) ion   (2 marks)

(b) When copper(II) carbonate is dissolved in the minimum quantity of concentrated hydrochloric acid, a yellow-brown solution is obtained. When water is added to this solution, the colour changes from yellow-brown through a variety of greens to the typical blue colour of aqueous copper(II) salts.

(i) Suggest a formula for the copper(II) complex in the yellow-brown
solution. (1 mark)

(ii) Explain why the colour changes upon the addition of water. (2 marks)

(c) Describe what would be observed in **each** of the following and write appropriate
equations for the reactions which occur.

(i) Aqueous potassium iodide is added to aqueous copper(II) sulphate (3 marks)

(ii) Aqueous ammonia is added to aqueous copper(II) sulphate (4 marks)

(d) Suggest the reagents and essential experimental conditions for a method that
might be used to prepare from metallic copper

(i) Copper(II) oxide (2 marks)

(ii) Copper(I) chloride (2 marks)

(total 16 marks)

Total mark for the paper: 75

PRACTICE PAPER 3 (1¼ hr) Organic chemistry

Question 1

(a) The diagram below represents a three-dimensional view of two molecules of
2-hydroxypropanoic acid.

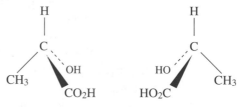

Molecule A   **Molecule B**

(i) What name is given to such molecules? (1 mark)

(ii) State **one** way in which the physical properties of a compound composed
entirely of molecule **A** would differ from a compound composed entirely
of molecule **B**. (2 marks)

(iii) What name would be given to an equi-molecular mixture of **A** and **B**?
(1 mark)

(b) Except for 2-aminoethanoic acid (glycine), the 2-aminoalkanoic acids are said to
exhibit *chirality*.

(i) Explain the meaning of *chirality*. (2 marks)

(ii) Draw the structural formulae for the isomers of the 2-aminoalkanoic acid
whose molecular formula is $C_3H_7NO_2$. (3 marks)

(c) Comment on the fact that the melting points of 2-aminoethanoic acid (rmm 75.1)
and propanoic acid (rmm 74.1) are $+262\,°C$ and $-21\,°C$ respectively. (3 marks)

(total 12 marks)

Question 2

2-bromopropane can react with hydroxide ions in two different ways.

$$\textbf{I} \quad (CH_3)_2CHBr + OH^- \rightarrow (CH_3)_2CHOH + Br^-$$

and $\quad \textbf{II} \quad (CH_3)_2CHBr + OH^- \rightarrow CH_3CH=CH_2 + Br^- + H_2O$

When 2-bromopropane is treated with sodium hydroxide, reactions **I** and **II** are
in competition and the degree to which one occurs in preference to the other
depends upon the reaction conditions.

(a) (i) What type of reaction takes place in reaction **I**? (1 mark)

(ii) What type of reaction has taken place in reaction **II**? (1 mark)

(iii) Which reaction is favoured by hot concentrated sodium hydroxide in
water/ethanol solution? (1 mark)

(b) (i) Draw the structure of the product formed when the compound with
formula $(CH_3)_2CHOH$, is oxidized with acidified aqueous potassium
dichromate(VI).   (1 mark)

(ii) Draw the structures of the two isomers formed when the compound with
formula $CH_3CH=CH_2$ is treated with bromine.   (2 marks)

(c) Write systematic names for the compounds **A**, **B** and **C** in the reaction scheme

(3 marks)
(total 9 marks)

Question 3
This question concerns aldehydes and ketones.
(a) Both aldehydes and ketones are carbonyl compounds that react with 2,4-dinitro-
phenylhydrazine by addition followed by elimination.
(i) Draw the structure of the functional group in an aldehyde and in a ketone.
(2 marks)
(ii) Draw the structural formula of 2,4-dinitrophenylhydrazine.   (1 mark)
(iii) Describe what is observed when a few drops of a liquid ketone are added
to the 2,4-dinitrophenylhydrazine reagent.   (1 mark)
(iv) Draw the structure of the product formed by the reaction of propanal with the
2,4-dinitrophenylhydrazine reagent.   (1 mark)
(v) Explain why the initial reaction of 2,4-dinitrophenylhydrazine with a
carbonyl compound is regarded as the addition of a nucleophile to an
electrophile.   (3 marks)
(b) Aldehydes can be distinguished from ketones by their reactions with reducing
agents such as sodium tetrahydridoborate(III) and by their reactions with oxidizing agents such as ammoniacal aqueous silver nitrate (Tollen's reagent).
(i) Draw a structure of the product in each case when sodium tetrahydrido-
borate(III) reacts separately with butanal and butanone.   (2 marks)
(ii) Describe what is seen when drops of butanal and butanone are added
separately to Tollen's reagent and the mixtures gently warmed.   (2 marks)
(total 12 marks)

Question 4
(a) Nicotine is an organic base and an extremely toxic constituent of the tobacco
plant. The compound has a molar mass of $162.23 \, g \, mol^{-1}$ and consists of carbon, hydrogen and nitrogen only. Combustion analysis of a 0.002500 g sample
of nicotine gave $6.782 \times 10^{-3} \, g$ of carbon dioxide and $1.9434 \times 10^{-3} \, g$ of
water. $(A_r(H) = 1.008; A_r(C) = 12.01; A_r(N) = 14.01; A_r(O) = 16.00)$
(i) Determine the molecular formula of nicotine.   (4 marks)
(ii) Suggest an explanation for the fact that one mole of nicotine can react
with one mole of hydrochloric acid.   (2 marks)
(b) Give the names of
(i) **two** techniques which can be used to purify an organic compound   (2 marks)
(ii) **two** physical techniques which can be used to investigate the structure of
a complex organic molecule   (2 marks)
(iii) **one** physical technique which can be used to analyse complex mixtures of
organic compounds   (1 mark)
(c) A white solid is thought to be benzoic acid. Describe a simple method for identi-
fying the solid as benzoic acid if a pure sample of benzoic acid is available.
(2 marks)
(total 13 marks)

Question 5
(a) Halogenation of monosubstituted benzene compounds is influenced by the reaction conditions and by the substituent attached to the benzene ring.
   (i) State the conditions needed for the chlorination of methylbenzene to form
      (chloromethyl)benzene, $C_6H_5CH_2Cl$.   (1 mark)
   (ii) State the conditions needed for the chlorination of methylbenzene to form
      2-chloromethylbenzene, $CH_3C_6H_4Cl$.   (1 mark)
   (iii) Give the name and structural formula of an isomer of
      2-chloromethylbenzene formed by chlorination of methylbenzene under
      the same conditions as in (ii).   (2 marks)
   (iv) Give the name and structural formula of the compound formed when
      phenol reacts with aqueous bromine.   (3 marks)
(b) Draw the structure and name the compounds produced by the hydrolysis of
   (i) (chloromethyl)benzene, $C_6H_5CH_2Cl$ (2 marks)
   (ii) (dichloromethyl)benzene, $C_6H_5CHCl_2$ (2 marks)
   (iii) (trichloromethyl)benzene, $C_6H_5CCl_3$ (2 marks)
                                    (total 13 marks)

Question 6
(a) Benzene reacts with concentrated nitric acid in the presence of concentrated
   sulphuric acid to form nitrobenzene. $C_6H_6 + HNO_3 \rightarrow C_6H_5NO_2 + H_2O$.
   (i) Give the name and formula of the ion which attacks the benzene ring in
      this reaction.   (2 marks)
   (ii) Show the mechanism by which the reaction takes place.   (2 marks)
   (iii) Classify the mechanism in (ii) above.   (1 mark)
   (iv) Explain why the temperature at which the reaction takes place must be
      kept below 55 °C.   (1 mark)
(b) Nitrobenzene can be reduced to phenylamine which can be diazotized and then
   coupled with phenol to form an azo dye.
   (i) Draw the structural formula of phenylamine.   (1 mark)
   (ii) State the reagents and reaction conditions needed to convert phenylamine
      into benzenediazonium chloride.   (3 marks)
(c) Draw the structure of the azo dye formed by the coupling reaction of phenol
   with benzenediazonium chloride.   (2 marks)
(d) Give the name of the product and write a balanced chemical equation for the
   reaction when benzenediazonium chloride is warmed with
   (i) aqueous potassium iodide   (2 marks)
   (ii) water   (2 marks)
                                      (total 16 marks)

Total mark for the paper: 75

PRACTICE PAPER 4 (1 hr) Objective test

Multiple choice questions

Summary of directions for multiple choice questions
Each question or incomplete statement is followed by four suggested answers labelled **A** to **D**. Select the **one** letter for the correct answer or best completing statement.

1 Which one of the following shapes would the VSEPR (valence shell electron pair repulsion) theory predict for germanium tetrachloride?
   A square planar   **C** tetrahedral
   B square pyramidal   **D** trigonal planar

2 Which one of the following atoms has two s electrons in its valence shell in the ground state configuration?

    A barium   **B** chromium   **C** copper   **D** sodium

3 Which one of the following has a zero dipole moment?

    A AlH_4^- **B** HCl **C** H_2O **D** NH_3

4 Which one of the following ions would have the greatest polarising power?

    A Li^+ **B** K^+ **C** Mg^{2+} **D** Al^{3+}

5 Which one of the following enthalpy changes is always negative?

    A atomization   **C** formation

    B bond dissociation   **D** neutralization

6 The standard enthalpy changes of formation (in $kJ\,mol^{-1}$) of zinc oxide and carbon monoxide are -348 and -111 respectively. What is the standard enthalpy change (in $kJ\,mol^{-1}$) for the reaction $ZnO + C \rightarrow Zn + CO$?

    A -459 **B** -237 **C** $+237$ **D** $+459$

7 What is the correct order of lattice energies, increasing from left to right, starting with the least exothermic?

    A $CaF_2 < CaCl_2 < NaCl$ **C** $NaCl < CaF_2 < CaCl_2$

    B $NaCl < CaCl_2 < CaF_2$ **D** $CaCl_2 < CaF_2 < NaCl$

8 The units of the rate constant for a second order reaction are

    A $mol\,dm^{-3}$ **B** $mol\,dm^{-3}\,s^{-1}$ **C** $mol^{-1}\,dm^3\,s^{-1}$ **D** $mol^2\,dm^{-6}\,s^{-1}$

9 The information in the table below refers to the reaction $X + Y \rightarrow$ products.

Experiment number	I	II	III
Initial concentration of **X** in $mol\,dm^{-3}$	0.1	0.1	0.2
Initial concentration of **Y** in $mol\,dm^{-3}$	0.1	0.2	0.2
Initial rate of reaction in arbitrary units	1	1	2

From the information it follows that

    A The reaction is second order overall.

    B The reaction is first order with respect to **Y**.

    C The rate constant has the units $mol\,dm^{-3}\,s^{-1}$.

    D The half-life for expt **I** is the same as for expt **III**.

10 Which one of the following statements is **FALSE**?

    A The pH = pOH in pure water.

    B The pH of pure water depends upon the temperature

    C The pH = pK_a in a weak acid/salt buffer when [weak acid] = [salt]

    D The pH > 7 in a buffer of ethanoic acid and sodium ethanoate

11 What would be the pH of hydrochloric acid of concentration $0.02\,mol\,dm^{-3}$?

    A 0.3   **B** 1.7   **C** 2.3   **D** 2.7

12 In the Haber process involving $3H_2(g) + N_2(g) \rightleftharpoons 2NH_3(g)$ where ΔH is negative, the yield of ammonia would be increased by

    A increasing the temperature at which equilibrium is reached

    B decreasing the total pressure at which equilibrium is reached

    C removing the ammonia as it forms

    D using an efficient catalyst

13 How many moles of electrons would be needed to reduce one mole of dichromate(VI) anions to chromium(III) cations?

    A 12   **B** 6   **C** 3   **D** $1\frac{1}{2}$

14 Copper displaces silver from aqueous silver nitrate. It follows that

    A silver ions are being reduced

    B silver atoms are being oxidized

    C a silver atom is a better reducing agent than a copper atom

    D a copper(II) ion is a better oxidizing agent than a silver ion

15 Which one of the following Group 4 chlorides is least easily hydrolysed?

    A CCl_4 **B** $SiCl_4$ **C** $SnCl_4$ **D** $PbCl_4$

16 Which one of the following will **not** give a precipitate with aqueous silver nitrate?

    A sodium fluoride   **C** sodium bromide

    B sodium chloride   **D** potassium iodide

17 How many isomers have the molecular formula C_5H_{12}?

    A 2   **B** 3   **C** 4   **D** 5

18 Which one of the following could **not** exhibit optical isomerism?

    A butan-2-ol   **C** 2-aminopropanoic acid

    B 2-methylpropane   **D** 2-hydroxypropanoic acid

19 Which one of the following would **not** give a carboxylic acid on refluxing with dilute hydrochloric acid?

    A methyl ethanoate   **C** propanamide

    B propanenitrile   **D** 2-aminopropane

20 Which one of the following represents an electrophile?

    A CN^- **B** $\cdot CH_3$ **C** NO_2^+ **D** OH^-

Grid questions

Summary of directions for answering grid questions
For each of the four questions (a)–(d) beneath the grid, write down the letter or letters chosen from **A–F** for the grid cells containing the correct answer or answers.

A	van der Waals forces and hydrogen bonding	**B**	covalent bonding	**C**	covalent bonding and hydrogen bonding
D	polar covalent bonding	**E**	coordinate (dative covalent) bonding	**F**	van der Waals forces

20 Identify the best description of the bonding forces between

    (a) water ligands and a copper ion in $[Cu(H_2O)_6]^{2+}$

    (b) a hydrogen atom and a chlorine atom in HCl

    (c) molecules in solid iodine

    (d) water molecules in ice

A	ΔG negative	**B**	ΔH negative	**C**	ΔS negative
D	ΔG positive	**E**	ΔH positive	**F**	ΔS positive

22 The grid refers to the terms in the relationship $\Delta G = \Delta H - T.\Delta S$

Identify the **one** term for a reaction that is

    (a) always feasible

    (b) exothermic

Identify the **three** terms that show a reaction to be

    (c) spontaneous and endothermic

    (d) exothermic and not feasible

A	zero order	**B**	first order	**C**	second order
D	$t_{1/2}$ is constant and independent of [ ]	**E**	$t_{1/2}$ is directly proportional to [ ]	**F**	$t_{1/2}$ is inversely proportional to [ ]

23 The grid refers to order and half-life ($t_{1/2}$) of a reaction. [ ] represents the concentration of a reactant. Identify the **two** which apply to

    (a) a reaction whose rate equation is $-d[\ ]/dt = k[\ ]$

    (b) a reaction whose rate is independent of the concentration of a reactant

    (c) the decay of a radioactive isotope

    (d) the hydrolysis of a bromoalkane by the S_N2 mechanism

A	K_c has the units $mol\,dm^{-3}$	B	K_c has no units	C	$K_p \neq K_c$
D	K_p has the units atm	E	K_p has no units	F	K_p decreases as temperature rises

24 Identify the statement(s) which would apply to the following reactions.

   (a) $2SO_2(g) + O_2(g) \rightleftharpoons 2SO_3(g)$; ΔH is negative

   (b) $H_2O(g) + CO(g) \rightleftharpoons H_2(g) + CO_2(g)$; ΔH is negative

   (c) $N_2O_4(g) \rightleftharpoons 2NO_2(g)$; ΔH is positive

   (d) $PCl_5(g) \rightleftharpoons PCl_3(g) + Cl_2(g)$; ΔH is positive

A	+1	B	+2	C	+3
D	+4	E	+6	F	+7

25 Identify the oxidation states for the **transition** elements in each of

   (a) $2Cu^{2+} + 4I^- \rightarrow 2CuI + I_2$

   (b) $VO^{2+} + 2H^+ + V^{2+} \rightarrow 2V^{3+} + H_2O$

   (c) $MnO_4^- + 8H^+ + 5Fe^{2+} \rightarrow Mn^{2+} + 4H_2O + 5Fe^{3+}$

   (d) $3MnO_4^{2-} + H_2O \rightarrow 2MnO_4^- + MnO_2 + 2OH^-$

A	sodium	B	lithium	C	barium
D	phosphorus	E	chlorine	F	fluorine

26 Identify the element which would
   (a) oxidize water
   (b) not react with water
   Identify the element(s) which would
   (c) be oxidized by water
   (d) form a sparingly soluble carbonate

A	$-CHO$	B	$-CO_2H$	C	$>CO$
D	$-CH_2OH$	E	$-COCl$	F	$-COC-$

27 Identify the functional group(s) which would
   (a) oxidize to a carboxylic acid   (c) react with a primary alcohol
   (b) react with aqueous carbonate   (d) react with phenylamine

Multiple completion questions

Summary of directions for answering multiple completion questions			
A	**B**	**C**	**D**
(i), (ii) and (iii) only	(i) and (iii) only	(ii) and (iv) only	(iv) only

28 Which attractive forces would operate between molecules in gaseous hydrogen fluoride?
   (i) van der Waals forces   (iii) hydrogen bonding
   (ii) permanent dipole   (iv) covalent bonding

29 Which of the following quantities would be involved in the Born-Haber cycle for the formation of sodium chloride?
(i) The electron affinity of chlorine
(ii) The first ionization energy of sodium
(iii) The enthalpy change of atomization of chlorine
(iv) The hydration enthalpy of the gaseous sodium ion

30 The following statements refer to a reaction whose energy profile is shown in the following diagram.

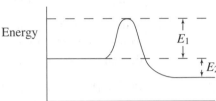

Reaction coordinate

Which of the statements would be correct?
(i) the activation energy for the forward reaction is $E_1 + E_2$
(ii) the enthalpy change for the forward reaction is $+E_2$
(iii) the enthalpy change for the reverse reaction is $-E_1$
(iv) the forward reaction is exothermic

31 In the nitric acid manufacture involving

$$4NH_3(g) + 5O_2(g) \rightleftharpoons 4NO(g) + 6H_2O(g) \text{ where } \Delta H = -1900 \text{ kJ mol}^{-1},$$

the percentage of unoxidized ammonia in the equilibrium mixture would be decreased by
(i) decreasing the temperature
(ii) increasing the total pressure
(iii) increasing the partial pressure of oxygen
(iv) using a platinum/rhodium catalyst

32 The standard electrode potential for $Cu^{2+}(aq)|Cu(s)$ is $+0.34$ volts and for $Zn^{2+}(aq)|Zn(s)$ is -0.76 volts. It follows that
(i) $Cu^{2+}(aq)$ is a stronger oxidizing agent than $Zn^{2+}(aq)$
(ii) $Zn(s)$ is a stronger reducing agent than $Cu(s)$
(iii) the standard e.m.f of a zinc/copper cell is $+1.10$ volts
(iv) the free energy change for $Zn(s) + Cu^{2+}(aq) \rightarrow Zn^{2+}(aq) + Cu(s)$ is positive

33 Which of the following characteristics of transition metals would **not** apply to zinc?
(i) element can exist in a variety of oxidation states
(ii) atoms and ions are paramagnetic
(iii) atoms have an incomplete 3d shell of electrons
(iv) metal readily forms alloys with other transition metals

34 Which of the following organic compounds would give a positive iodoform test?
(i) ethanol   (iii) propan-2-ol
(ii) methanol   (iv) propan-1-ol

Total mark for the paper: 55

SOLUTIONS TO PRACTICE PAPER 1

Question 1
(a) (i) $CO_3^{2-}(aq)$, $SO_3^{2-}(aq)$ and $SO_4^{2-}(aq)$ *(2 marks)*
   (ii) $SO_4^{2-}(aq)$ *(1 mark)*
(b) $[Al(H_2O)_6]^{3+}(aq)$, $[Zn(H_2O)_4]^{2+}(aq)$ and $[Pb(H_2O)_4]^{2+}(aq)$ *(2 marks)*
(c) (i) When the blue aqueous copper(II) sulphate is added to the colourless aqueous potassium iodide, the mixture turns brown and a white precipitate appears. $4I^-(aq) + 2Cu^{2+}(aq) \rightarrow I_2(aq) + 2CuI(s)$.   *(3 marks)*

(ii) When the purple acidified aqueous potassium manganate(VII) is added to the colourless aqueous potassium iodide, the purple colour is replaced by a yellow colour which gradually becomes dark brown as more aqueous potassium manganate(VII) is added. A grey-black precipitate is formed when excess aqueous potassium manganate(VII) is added.

$$MnO_4^-(aq) + 8H^+(aq) + 15I^-(aq) \rightarrow Mn^{2+}(aq) + 4H_2O(l) + 5I_3^-(aq)$$

$$I_3^-(aq) \rightarrow I_2(s) + I^-(aq)$$ *(3 marks)*

(d) (i) When the colourless aqueous ammonia is added to the pale-green aqueous iron(II) sulphate, a green gelatinous precipitate is formed which begins to darken and, on the surface of the mixture, to turn brown.

$$Fe^{2+}(aq) + 2OH^-(aq) \rightarrow Fe(OH)_2(s)$$

$$2Fe(OH)_2(s) + H_2O(l) + \tfrac{1}{2}O_2(aq) \rightarrow 2Fe(OH)_3(s)$$ *(2 marks)*

(ii) When the purple acidified aqueous potassium manganate(VII) is added to the pale-green aqueous iron(II) sulphate, the purple colour is replaced by a yellow colour.

$$MnO_4^-(aq) + 8H^+(aq) + 2\tfrac{1}{2}Fe^{2+}(aq) \rightarrow$$
$$Mn^{2+}(aq) + 4H_2O(l) + 2\tfrac{1}{2}Fe^{3+}(aq)\ \textit{(2 marks)}$$

(e) (i) $2S_2O_3^{2-}(aq) + I_2(aq) \rightarrow S_4O_6^{2-}(aq) + 2I^-(aq)$ *(2 marks)*
(ii) $(0.0105 \times 2 \times 21.5)/25.0 = 0.0181\ mol\,dm^{-3}\ I_2(aq)$.   *(2 marks)*
(total 19 marks)

Question 2
(a) (i) hexagonal close-packed and cubic close-packed   *(2 marks)*
(ii) the coordination number of an atom (or ion) in a metallic crystal structure is the number of nearest equidistant neighbouring atoms (or ions). Value = 12
                                                                                      (2 marks)

(iii) coordination number = 8

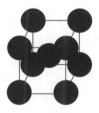

                                                                                      (2 marks)
(b) (i) The transition metal atoms are similar in size and have small atomic radii.
                                                                                      (1 mark)
(ii) Nickel and chromium form *nichrome*   *(3 marks)*
(iii) Used in electrical components because its resistance changes very little with temperature.   *(2 marks)*
(c) (i) *non-stoichiometric* means not having a constant composition by mass.
                                                                                      (1 mark)

(ii) An *interstitial compound* is one in which small atoms (of elements such as hydrogen, carbon and nitrogen) occupy spaces (interstices) in the metallic crystal lattice (usually of a transition element).   *(2 marks)*
(total 15 marks)

Question 3
(a) *colorimetry* (measuring the change in the intensity of a coloured reactant/product)
dilatometry (measuring the change in volume of the reaction mixture)
polarimetry (measuring the change in the angle of rotation of an optically active component in the reaction mixture)   *(3 marks)*
(b) (i) First order   *(1 mark)*
(ii) $(CH_3)_3CBr \rightarrow (CH_3)_3C^+ + Br^-$ *(1 mark)*

(iii) The carbocation $(CH_3)_3C^+$ is unstable and would be attracted to the oppositely charged hydroxide ion, OH^-. *(1 mark)*

(c) (i) The reciprocal $(1/t)$ of the time *(1 mark)*

(ii) So that the concentrations of the other two reactants will stay (almost) unchanged (because only small amounts are used up) and therefore their effect upon the rate will be constant. Any change in the rate will be due to a change in the concentration of the reactant being studied. *(1 mark)*

(iii) $rate = k[H_2O_2(aq)][I^-(aq)]$ *(2 marks)*

(iv) Doubling the hydrogen peroxide concentration would double the rate. Doubling the iodide ion concentration would also double the rate. Doubling both at the same time would quadruple the rate. Changing the concentration of the hydrogen ion would have no effect on the rate. *(2 marks)*

(total 12 marks)

Question 4

(a) Place measured amounts of the ester and water, together with a small measured amount of concentrated sulphuric acid (as catalyst), into a glass flask. Tightly stopper the flask and leave the mixture in a constant temperature bath at $50\,^\circ C$ to reach equilibrium. Titrate the contents of the flask with aqueous sodium hydroxide of known concentration using phenolphthalein (colourless to pink) as indicator. Allowing for the sulphuric acid, find the amount of ethanoic acid (= amount of ethanol) formed at equilibrium and, by difference from the initial amounts, find the equlibrium amounts of ester and water. Hence calculate a value for the constant. *(5 marks)*

(b) equilibrium amount of ester = equilibrium amount of water = $0.845\,mol$
equilibrium amount of ethanoic acid is $2 - 0.845 = 1.155\,mol$
equilibrium amount of ethanol is $1 - 0.845 = 0.155\,mol$
equlibrium constant value is $(0.845 \times 0.845)/(1.155 \times 0.155) = K_c = 3.99$
(4 marks)

(c) (i) High pressure would have no effect upon the composition of the equilibrium mixture (moles reactant gases = moles product gases) but high pressure would increase solubility of carbon dioxide in water. *(2 marks)*

(ii) A lower temperature would increase the partial pressures of carbon dioxide and hydrogen in the equilibrium mixture (because the reaction is exothermic) but the rate of attainment of equilibrium would be slower. *(2 marks)*

(iii) $-8.27\,kJ\,mol^{-1} = -\{(8.31\,J\,K^{-1}\,mol^{-1})/1000\} \times 800\,K \times \ln K_p$
Hence, $\ln K_p = 1.24$ and $K_p = 3.47$ *(2 marks)*

(total 15 marks)

Question 5

(a) (i) $Cr^{2+}(aq)$ *(1 mark)*

(ii) $Pt\,|\,[2Cr^{3+}(aq) + 7H_2O(l)],[Cr_2O_7^{2-}(aq) + 14H^+(aq)] \vdots\vdots Cr^{3+}(aq),Cr^{2+}(aq)\,|\,Pt$ *(1 mark)*

(iii) $(+1.33) - (-0.41) = 1.74\,V$. The dichromate(VI) electrode is positive. *(1 mark)*

(iv) $Cr_2O_7^{2-}(aq) + 14H^+(aq) + 6Cr^{2+}(aq) \rightarrow 8Cr^{3+}(aq) + 7H_2O(l)$ *(1 mark)*

(v) The standard reduction potential for zinc $(-0.76\,V)$ compared with that for the chromium(II) ion $(-0.41\,V)$ means that zinc is the stronger reducing agent. *(1 mark)*

(vi) $Cr_2O_7^{2-}(aq) + 14H^+(aq) + 4Zn(s) \rightarrow 2Cr^{2+}(aq) + 7H_2O(l) + 4Zn^{2+}(aq)$ *(1 mark)*

(vii) Air must be kept out to avoid the chromium(II) being oxidized to chromium(III) by oxygen. For example:

$O_2(g) + 4H^+(aq) + 4Cr^{2+}(aq) \rightarrow 4Cr^{3+}(aq) + 2H_2O(l)$ *(2 marks)*

(b) (i) CrO_4^{2-}(aq)   *(1 mark)*

(ii) $2CrO_4^{2-}$(aq) + $2H^+$(aq) $\rightleftharpoons$ $Cr_2O_7^{2-}$(aq) + H_2O(l)   *(2 marks)*

(iii) The yellow solution turns orange-red because the increase in the concentration of H^+(aq) ions causes the concentration of the CrO_4^{2-}(aq) to fall and that of the $Cr_2O_7^{2-}$(aq) to rise according to the law of chemical equilibrium.   *(2 marks)*

(iv) Barium chromate(VI) is less soluble than barium dichromate(VI). When barium chromate(VI) precipitates and the concentration of the CrO_4^{2-}(aq) falls, more $Cr_2O_7^{2-}$(aq) ions turn into CrO_4^{2-}(aq) as the reaction shifts from right to left according to the law of chemical equilibrium.   *(2 marks)*

(total 15 marks)

Question 6

(a) (i) To prevent the coal burning (mainly to carbon dioxide and water)   *(1 mark)*

(ii) Methane   *(1 mark)*

(iii) Unlike carbon monoxide, methane is not poisonous. The risk of an explosion with methane–air mixtures is lower than that with hydrogen–air mixtures.

(2 marks)

(iv) 50% H_2 + 32% CH_4 + 8% CO + 4% C_2H_4 + 6% N_2
$0.50 \times 2.016 + 0.32 \times (12.01+4.032) + 0.08 \times (12.01+16.00) + 0.04 \times (24.02+4.032) + 0.06 \times (28.02) = 11.19 \, g \, mol^{-1}$ is average molar mass of coal-gas.   *(2 marks)*

(v) Molar volume at 298 K (= 25.0 °C) is $22.4 \times 298/273 = 24.5 \, dm^3 \, mol^{-1}$
So, density of coal gas is $11.19 \, g \, mol^{-1} \div 24.5 \, dm^3 \, mol^{-1} = 0.457 \, g \, dm^{-3}$

(2 marks)

(b) (i) Ca(s) + H_2(g) → CaH_2(s)   *(1 mark)*

(ii) $Ca^{2+}(H^-)_2$ (ionic bonding)   *(1 mark)*

(iii) CaH_2(s) + $2H_2O$(l) → $Ca(OH)_2$(s) + $2H_2$(g)   *(1 mark)*

(iv) Twice as much hydrogen is liberated from one mole of calcium hydride as is taken up to form one mole of calcium hydride so the compound, if kept dry, might be a useful and compact way of storing hydrogen.   *(2 marks)*

(v) Combustion of methane may release more heat than the combustion of the same volume of hydrogen measured at the same temperature and pressure.

(1 mark)

(total 14 marks)

Total mark for the paper: 90

SOLUTIONS TO PRACTICE PAPER 2

Question 1

(a) (i) Cu [argon core] 3d [↑↓][↑↓][↑↓][↑↓][↑↓] 4s [↑]
Fe^{2+} [argon core] 3d [↑↓][↑][↑][↑][↑] 4s [ ]
Fe^{3+} [argon core] 3d [↑][↑][↑][↑][↑] 4s [ ]   *(3 marks)*

(ii) The greater stability of the iron(III) ion compared with the iron(II) ion reflects the greater stability of a 3d shell with each orbital containing 1 electron compared with the arrangement shown for the Fe^{2+} ion.   *(2 marks)*

(b) (i) The forces holding the Group 2 cations and chloride anions together in the crystal will decrease because the charge density of the cations decreases as their radii increase. It follows that the lattice-breaking enthalpy decreases (becomes less positive).   *(2 marks)*

(ii) The polarizing power of the Group 2 cations will decrease because the charge density of the cations decreases as their radii increase. It follows that the enthalpy of formation of the hydrated cations decreases (becomes less negative). *(2 marks)*

(iii) The solubility of the sulphates decreases with increasing atomic number because the hydration enthalpy becomes less able to compensate for the lattice-breaking enthalpy. *(2 marks)*

(c) (i) boron B $1s^2 2s^2 2p^1$ nitrogen N $1s^2 2s^2 2p^3$ *(2 marks)*

(ii)

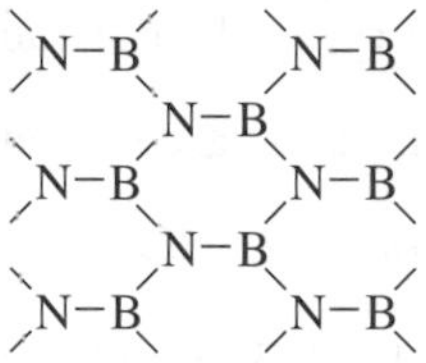

(2 marks)

(total 15 marks)

Question 2

(a) A nitrogen atom has a ground state electronic configuration of $1s^2 2s^2 2p^3$ and it can only accept three electrons to complete its outer shell. A phosphorus atom has a ground state electronic configuration of $1s^2 2s^2 2p^6 3s^2 3p^3$ so it can accept three electrons to fill the 3p orbitals and also accept two electrons into 3d orbitals to extend the outer shell beyond 8 electrons. *(2 marks)*

(b) **Vapour**   **Solid**

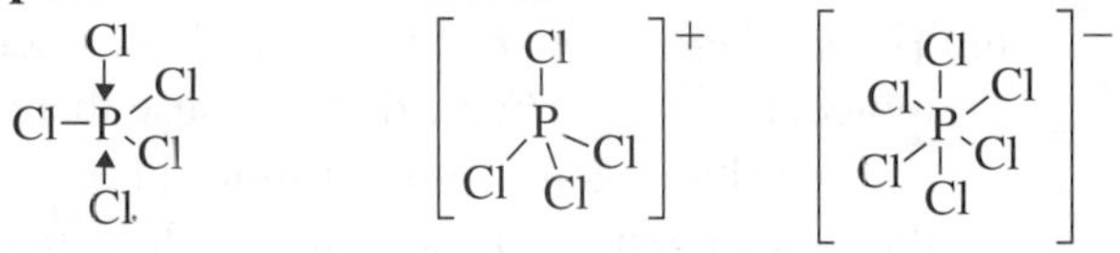

bipyramidal   tetrahedral   octahedral   *(3 marks)*

(c)

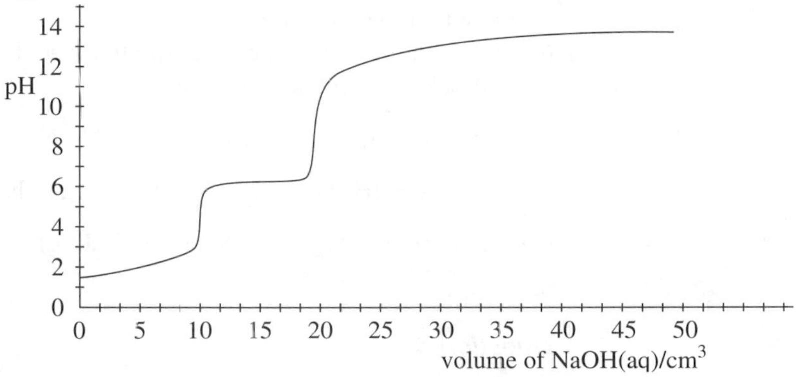

volume of NaOH(aq)/cm^3 *(4 marks)*

(d) (i) All four hydride molecules have a pyramidal structure due to the repulsion between the lone pair of electrons and the three bonded electron pairs.

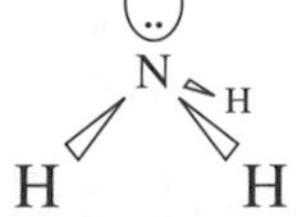

(2 marks)

(ii) The H—N—H bond angle is almost the tetrahedral angle because the attraction of the highly electronegative nitrogen atom for the three bonded electron pairs enhances their mutual repulsions and consequently diminishes the repulsive effect of the lone pair of electrons. The electronegativity of the Group 5 elements decreases with increasing atomic number and consequently the bond angle decreases. *(2 marks)*

(iii) The basic strength of the hydrides decreases with increasing atomic number and decreasing electronegativity of the Group 5 elements as the lone pair of electrons is less readily donated to form a bond with the proton from the acid. *(2 marks)*

(iv) The N—H bond is the shortest and strongest. With increasing atomic number, the bond to hydrogen becomes longer and weaker so the thermal stability decreases down the group. *(2 marks)*

(total 17 marks)

Question 3

(a) (i)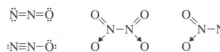

(2 marks)

(ii) In their molecular structures the nitrogen atom has an unpaired electron.
·NO and ·NO$_2$ (2 marks)

(iii) Equation: $2NO_2(g) + 2NaOH(aq) \rightarrow NaNO_2(aq) + NaNO_3(aq) + H_2O(l)$

Type of reaction: acid–base or neutralization   (2 marks)

(b) Equation: $2KNO_3(s) \rightarrow 2KNO_2(s) + O_2(g)$

Name of products: potassium nitrite or potassium nitrate(III) and oxygen

Equation: $2Cu(NO_3)_2(s) \rightarrow 2CuO(s) + 4NO_2(g) + O_2(g)$

Name of products: copper(II) oxide, nitrogen dioxide and oxygen   (4 marks)

(c) (i) -2 *(1 mark)*   (ii)

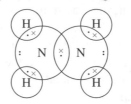

(1 mark)

(iii) The *average number* of hydrogen bonds per molecule that can form between
molecules is 2 for hydrazine (because there are two lone pairs of electrons
and four hydrogen atoms per molecule), 1 for ammonia (because there are
three hydrogen atoms but only one lone pair of electrons per molecule) and 0
for phosphine (because the electronegativity of phosphorus is too low to pro-
mote hydrogen bonding).   (3 marks)

(iv) Hydrazine is a di-acidic base, sulphuric acid is a di-basic acid and
hydrochloric acid is monobasic:

$$H_2N-NH_2(aq) + H_2SO_4(aq) \rightarrow {}^{+}H_3N-NH_3^{+}(aq) + SO_4^{2-}(aq)$$

and $H_2N-NH_2(aq) + 2HCl(aq) \rightarrow {}^{+}H_3N-NH_3^{+}(aq) + 2Cl^{-}(aq)$ (2 marks)

(v) $2N_2H_4(l) + N_2O_4(l) \rightarrow 3N_2(g) + 4H_2O(g)$ (1 mark)

(total 18 marks)

Question 4

(a) (i) $PCl_3(l) + 3H_2O(l) \rightarrow H_3PO_3(aq) + 3HCl(aq)$ (1 mark)

(ii) NaH_2PO_3 and Na_2HPO_3 (1 mark)

(iii) $H_3PO_3(aq) + Cu^{2+}(aq) + H_2O(l) \rightarrow H_3PO_4(aq) + Cu(s) + 2H^{+}(aq)$
                                                                                (2 marks)

(iv)

H—O   H
   \ /
    P
   / ‖
H—O   O   (1 mark)

(b) $100\,cm^3$ of $1.0\,mol\,dm^{-3}$ HCl $\equiv 50\,cm^3$ of $2.0\,mol\,dm^{-3}$ NaOH so,
$(150 - 50) = 100\,cm^3$ of $2.0\,mol\,dm^{-3}$ NaOH $\equiv 0.20\,mol$ reacted with
fertilizer.

$2NaOH(aq) + (NH_4)_2SO_4(aq) \rightarrow Na_2SO_4(aq) + 2H_2O(l) + 2NH_3(g)$

2 mol   1 mol
0.2 mol   0.1 mol $0.1 \times \{2 \times (14+4) + 32 + 4 \times 16\} = 13.2\,g$
So, % by mass in 15 g is $100 \times 13.2/15 = 88\%$ ammonium sulphate. *(4 marks)*

(total 9 marks)

Question 5

(a) (i) Cu atom $1s^22s^22p^63s^23p^63d^{10}4s^1$ *(1 mark)*

(ii) Cu^{2+} ion $1s^22s^22p^63s^23p^63d^9$ *(1 mark)*

(b) (i) $CuCl_4^{2-}$ *(1 mark)*

(ii) The tetrachlorocuprate(II) complex anion reacts with water molecules to form the tetraaquacopper(II) complex cation whose aqueous solution is blue.

$$CuCl_4^{2-}(aq) + 4H_2O(l) \rightleftharpoons [Cu(H_2O)_4]^{2+}(aq) + 4Cl^-(aq)$$

The green colours correspond to solutions containing mixtures of the complex anion and complex cation. *(2 marks)*

(c) (i) When the colourless aqueous potassium iodide is added to the blue aqueous copper(II) sulphate, the mixture turns brown and a white precipitate appears.

$$4I^-(aq) + 2Cu_2+(aq) \rightarrow I_2(aq) + 2CuI(s).$$ *(3 marks)*

(ii) When the colourless aqueous ammonia is added to the blue aqueous copper(II) sulphate, a blue precipitate appears at first but disappears (when excess ammonia is added) to leave a deep blue solution.

$$2OH^-(aq) + Cu^{2+}(aq) \rightarrow Cu(OH)_2(s) \text{ then}$$

$$4NH_3(aq) + Cu(OH)_2(s) \rightarrow [Cu(NH_3)_4]^{2+}(aq)$$ *(4 marks)*

(d) (i) Concentrated nitric acid (to form a solution of copper(II) nitrate) followed by heating (to evaporate the solution to dryness and decompose the salt) *(2 marks)*

(ii) Copper(II) oxide (prepared as above) and concentrated hydrochloric acid (to form a solution of a copper(II) chloride complex) followed by mixing and heating with metallic copper (to form a solution of a copper(I) chloride complex) then pouring into cold air-free water *(2 marks)*

(total 16 marks)

Total mark for the paper: 75

SOLUTIONS TO PRACTICE PAPER 3

Question 1

(a) (i) Enantiomers (or optical isomers) *(1 mark)*

(ii) Rotation of the plane of polarized light by (crystals or a solution of) molecule **A** would be in the opposite direction to that by molecule **B** *(2 marks)*

(iii) A racemic mixture *(1 mark)*

(b) (i) Chirality (Greek: *cheir* – hand) refers to right- and left-handedness. A chiral molecule is not identical with its mirror image. Molecule **A** and molecule **B** have mirror-image structures that cannot be superimposed. The carbon atom with the four different atoms or groups (H, OH, CH_3, CO_2H) attached is called a chiral centre. *(2 marks)*

(ii)

(3 marks)

(c) Propanoic acid molecules are hydrogen-bonded into dimers:

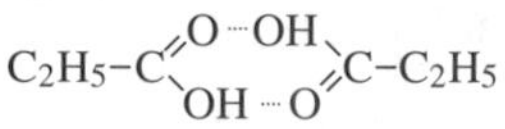

$$C_2H_5-C\overset{O\cdots OH}{\underset{OH\cdots O}{}}C-C_2H_5$$

Weak van der Waals forces hold the dimeric molecules together in the low-melting point solid.

In 2-aminoethanoic acid, the carboxyl group loses its proton to the amino group to form 'zwitterions' ($^+H_3NCH_2CO_2^-$) that are held together in the high-melting point solid by the electrostatic forces of ion–ion interactions. *(3 marks)*

(total 12 marks)

Question 2

(a) (i) **I** – nucleophilic substitution *(1 mark)*

(ii) **II** – addition/elimination (dehydrohalogenation) *(1 mark)*

(iii) reaction **II** *(1 mark)*

(b) (i)

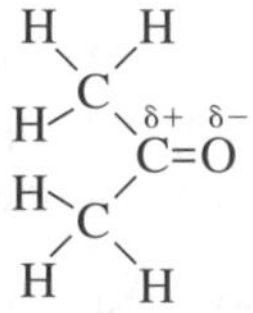

(1 mark)

(ii)

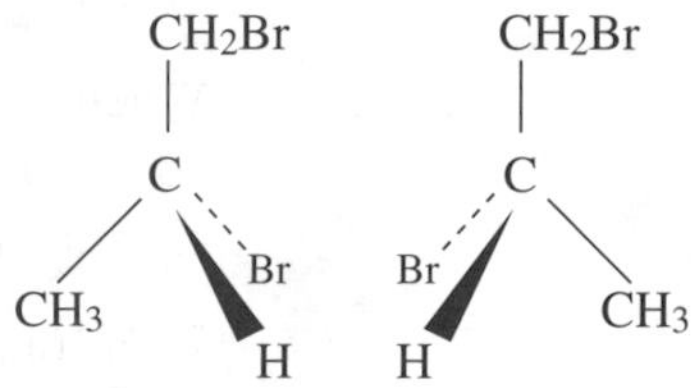

(2 marks)

(c) **A** bromoethane

B propanenitrile

C propanoic acid *(3 marks)*

(total 9 marks)

Question 3

(a) (i)

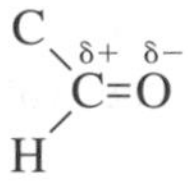

aldehyde 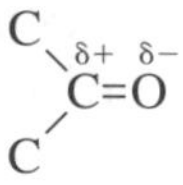   ketone *(2 marks)*

(ii)

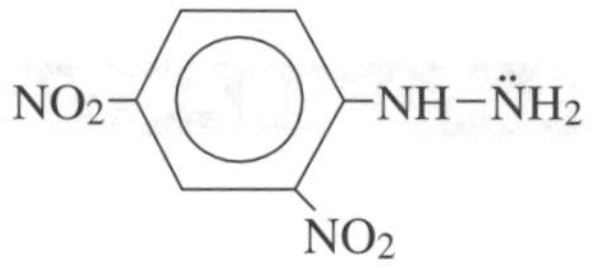

(1 mark)

(iii) A yellow-orange crystalline precipitate forms. *(1 mark)*

(iv)

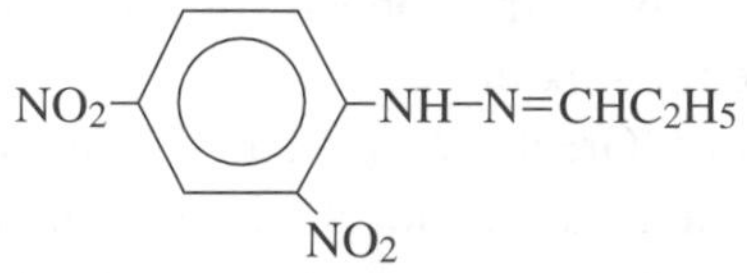

(1 mark)

(v) The lone pair of electrons on the nitrogen atom can form a dative bond with the carbonyl carbon atom made electrophilic by the electronegative oxygen atom doubly bonded to it.

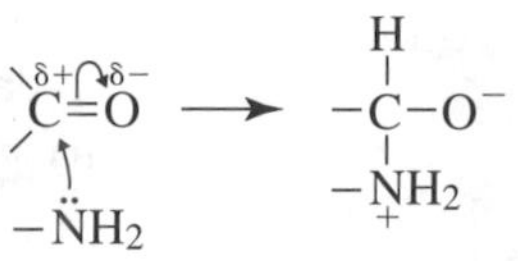

(3 marks)

(b) (i) from butanal

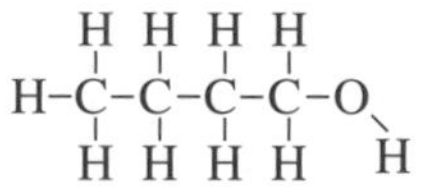

from butanone

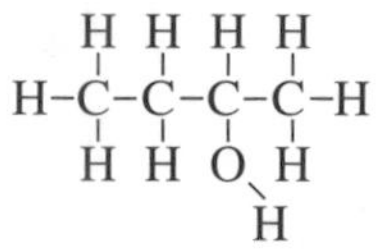

(2 marks)

(ii) A silver mirror or a black precipitate of metallic silver is formed with butanal. The butanone does not react but may form a milky emulsion.

(2 marks)

(total 12 marks)

Question 4

(a) (i) molar mass CO_2 is $12.01 + 2 \times 16.00 = 44.01\,\text{g mol}^{-1}$
molar mass H_2O is $2 \times 1.008 + 16.00 = 18.016\,\text{g mol}^{-1}$
$0.002500\,\text{g}$ is $0.002500/162.23 = 1.541 \times 10^{-5}\,\text{mol nicotine}$
$6.782 \times 10^{-3}\,\text{g}\ CO_2$ contains $(6.782 \times 10^{-3})/44.01 = 1.541 \times 10^{-4}\,\text{mol C}$
or $1.541 \times 10^{-4} \times 12.01 = 0.001851\,\text{g carbon}$
$1.9434 \times 10^{-3}\,\text{g}\ H_2O$ contains $2 \times (1.9434 \times 10\text{-}3)/18.016$
$= 2.157 \times 10^{-4}\,\text{mol H}$
or $2.157 \times 10^{-4} \times 1.008 = 0.000217\,\text{g hydrogen}$
$0.002500 - (0.001851 + 0.000217) = 0.000432\,\text{g nitrogen}$
or $3.084 \times 10^{-5}\,\text{mol N}$ contained in $1.541 \times 10^{-5}\,\text{mol nicotine}$
so, 1 mol nicotine contains $(1.541 \times 10^{-4})/1.541 \times 10^{-5} = 10\,\text{mol C atoms}$
$(2.157 \times 10^{-4})/1.541 \times 10^{-5} = 14\,\text{mol H atoms}$
$(3.084 \times 10^{-5})/1.541 \times 10^{-5} = 2\,\text{mol N atoms}$
so, molecular formula of nicotine is $C_{10}H_{14}N_2$. *(4 marks)*

(ii) The molecule contains one nitrogen atom capable of acting as a Lewis base because it has a lone pair of electrons. $\equiv N\!: + H\!-\!Cl \rightarrow \equiv N\!:\!H^+ + Cl^-$
(2 marks)

(b) (i) Crystallization and distillation *(2 marks)*
(ii) X-ray diffraction and infra-red spectroscopy *(2 marks)*
(iii) Chromatography *(1 mark)*

(c) Measure separately the melting point of the white solid and of the pure sample of benzoic acid. Mix the white solid with some of the pure sample of benzoic acid and measure the melting point of the mixture. If the white solid is benzoic acid, all three melting points should be the same. *(2 marks)*
(total 13 marks)

Question 5

(a) (i) Pass chlorine gas into the liquid exposed to ultraviolet light or bright sunshine and boiled under reflux. *(1 mark)*
(ii) Pass chlorine gas into the liquid mixed with iodine or iron filings (or iron(III) chloride) as a halogen carrier and boiled under reflux. *(1 mark)*
(iii) 4-chloromethylbenzene (iv) 2,4,6-tribromophenol

(2 marks) *(3 marks)*

(b) (i) benzyl alcohol (ii) benzaldehyde (iii) benzoic acid

(6 marks)
(total 13 marks)

Question 6

(a) (i) nitronium (or nitryl) ion NO_2^+ *(2 marks)*
(ii)

(2 marks)

(iii) Electrophilic substitution   *(1 mark)*

(iv) To avoid the formation of 2,4-dinitrobenzene made by further nitration.

                                                   (1 mark)

(b) (i)

NH_2

(ii) phenylamine dissolved in hydrochloric acid and the solution kept between $0\,°C$ and $5\,°C$ during the addition of a slight excess aqueous sodium nitrite   *(4 marks)*

(c)

—N=N—〇—OH

                                               (2 marks)

(d) (i) Iodobenzene $C_6H_5N_2Cl + KI \rightarrow C_6H_5I + KCl + N_2$ *(2 marks)*

    (ii) Phenol $C_6H_5N_2Cl + H_2O \rightarrow C_6H_5OH + HCl + N_2$ *(2 marks)*

                                             (total 16 marks)

Total mark for the paper: 75

SOLUTIONS TO PRACTICE PAPER 4

Multiple choice answers

1	C	5	D	9	D	13	B	17	B
2	A	6	C	10	D	14	A	18	B
3	A	7	B	11	B	15	A	19	D
4	D	8	C	12	C	16	A	20	C

Grid answers

Grid 21	*Grid 22*	*Grid 23*	*Grid 24*	*Grid 25*	*Grid 26*	*Grid 27*
(a) E	(a) A	(a) BD	(a) F	(a) BA	(a) F	(a) AD
(b) D	(b) B	(b) AE	(b) BEF	(b) DBC	(b) D	(b) BE
(c) F	(c) AEF	(c) BD	(c) ADC	(c) FBC	(c) ABC	(c) BE
(d) A	(d) DBC	(d) CF	(d) ADC	(d) EFB	(d) BC	(d) E

Multiple completion answers

28	29	30	31	32	33	34
A	A	D	B	A	C	B

Total mark for the paper: 55